SOCIAL CHANGE IN WESTERN EUROPE

LONG-TERM UNEMPLOYMENT

The *Social Change in Western Europe* series developed from the need to provide a summary of current thinking from leading academic thinkers on major social and economic issues concerning the evolving policies of Western Europe in the post-Maastricht era. To create an effective European Union governments and politicians throughout the region must work to provide satisfactory social, economic and political conditions for the populations of Europe, and each volume affords an opportunity to look at specific issues and their impact on individual countries.

The series is directed by an academic committee composed of Arnaldo Bagnasco (Turin University), Henri Mendras (CNRS, Paris) and Vincent Wright (Nuffield, Oxford), assisted by Patrick Le Galès (CNRS, Rennes), Anand Menon (University of Oxford) with the support of Michel Roger and Olivier Cazenave (Futuroscope in Poitiers). This group forms the *Observatoire du Changement en Europe Occidentale* which was launched in Poitiers (France) in 1990 with the generous funding of the Foundation de Poitiers headed by René Monory.

SOCIAL CHANGE IN WESTERN EUROPE

SOCIAL CHANGE IN WESTERN EUROPE

LONG-TERM UNEMPLOYMENT

edited by
ODILE BENOIT-GUILBOT
and
DUNCAN GALLIE

PINTER
PUBLISHERS

DISTRIBUTED IN THE USA AND CANADA BY ST. MARTIN'S PRESS

Pinter Publishers

25 Floral Street, Covent Garden, London, WC2E 9DS, United Kingdom

First published in Great Britain in 1994

© Actes Sud 1994

Distributed in the USA and Canada by St. Martin's Press, Inc., Room 400, 175 Fifth Avenue, New York, NY10010, USA

British Library Cataloguing in Publication Data

A CIP catalogue record for this book is available from The British Library

ISBN 1 85567 248 O (hb)
    1 85567 212 X (pb)

Library of Congress Cataloging-in-Publication Data

A CIP catalog record for this title is available from The Library of Congress

Typeset by Florencetype Ltd, Kewstoke, Avon
Printed and bound in Great Britain

CONTENTS

LIST OF CONTRIBUTORS

Odile Benoît-Guilbot is Director of Research at CNRS (*Observatoire sociologique du Changement*/FNSP). She has recently edited the special number on unemployment published by *Sociologie du travail* (vol. 32, no. 4, 1990).

Mireille Clémençon is direcor of studies at CNRS.

Duncan Gallie, Official Fellow of Nuffield College, Oxford, specialises in the labour market and in social attitudes in Britain and France. His most recently published work is *Employment in Britain* (Blackwell, Oxford, 1988).

Paul de Graaf is associate professor of sociology at the University of Nijmegen.

Emilio Reyneri is a professor at the University of Parma. His work has been directed in particular at neo-corporatist regulation of the labour market and at unemployment in Italy.

Helmut Rudolph is a researcher at the Institut fur Arbeitsmarkt und Berufsforschung in Nuremberg. He specialises in longitudinal analyses of employment and unemployment.

Luis Toharia is a professor at the University of Alcalà (ESA Foundation) in Madrid. As an economist, he has made a study of the labour market in Spain in collaboration with OECD.

Wout C. Ultee is Professor of Sociology at the Sociologish Institut, Kathe Leike Universiteit, Nijmegen. He has studied social classes and the labour market and culture in the Netherlands. His most recently published work (with J. Dessens and W. Jansen) is *Stratificaring 1974–1988* (Organisatie voor strategisch Arbeidsmarktonderzoek, The Hague, 1990).

Christopher T. Whelan is Director of Research at the Economical Social Research Institute in Dublin. His most recently published work (with D. Hanman and S. Creighton) is *Unemployment, Poverty and Psychological Distress* (ESRI, Dublin, 1991).

Michael White is Director of Research at the Policy Studies Institute in London. His field of study is the labour market and unemployment in Britain. His most recently published work is *Against Unemployment* (PSI, London, 1991).

INTRODUCTION: WHY ARE THERE SO MANY LONG-TERM UNEMPLOYED IN THE EU?

Odile Benoît-Guilbot

In Europe it has become customary for the media to sensationalise the publication of monthly unemployment rates. Any deterioration arouses dismay and anxiety; any improvement is greeted with relief and encouragement. The overall figures for unemployment have taken on symbolic value capable of making or unmaking political majorities of whatever colour. In spite of their paramount importance in the fight against unemployment the figures for long-term unemployment, that is to say unemployment of more than a year's duration, are given an altogether lower profile. Yet they represent a blight that, among developed countries, particularly affects those of the EU. It is a tragedy for the victims and a scandal for rich societies, whose wealth is attributable to work and for whom the right to work is recognised as a fundamental right; a scandal capable of undermining their foundations, even if degrees of financial compensation granted by governments mitigate the consequences of the lack of employment.

   A first look at unemployment of less than a year's duration, which provides an approximate measure of those entering unemployment, shows that there is little divergence between the countries of the European Union and those of the OECD (apart from Japan); neither group is markedly differentiated by short-term unemployment, and variations in the short-term unemployment rate are slight. Inflow into unemployment is as great – sometimes less so – in the EU[1] as in North America. Spain and Canada hold the record for unemployment of less than a year's duration with a rate of 7 per cent of the labour force.[2] Ireland and France follow with a rate of 5.8 per cent and 5.3 per cent respectively; then Australia, the USA, Norway, the Netherlands and Great Britain (from 4.9 per cent to 4.2 per cent). Finally come Italy, Federal Germany, Portugal, Belgium and Sweden (from 3.2 per cent to

1.3 per cent). Variations range from 1.3 per cent to 7 per cent. So as regards unemployment of less than a year's duration, in the sense of inflows into unemployment, the European countries are no different from other OECD countries.

What distinguishes Europe of the EU is the continuing length of unemployment. Once on the labour market job applicants appear to have enormous trouble finding or returning to work. The proportion of unemployed who remain so for a year or more is a lot higher than in the other OECD countries. Long-term unemployment almost everywhere in the EC withstood the slight upturn in employment which was apparent from 1983 onwards. In 1989, for instance, in EC countries unemployed of more than a year's standing represented between 41 per cent and 76 per cent of overall unemployed, whereas among other OECD countries the figure was 6 per cent or 7 per cent in Canada, the USA and Sweden, 12 per cent in Norway and 23 per cent in Australia. The difference is considerable and systematic.

Long-term unemployment results from the successive build-up over a period of years of unemployed who have been unable to achieve entry or re-entry into employment. To take France, 13 per cent of one cohort of entrants were still unemployed 12 months later (SES, 1990; 1989 cohort); in Britain, according to Daniel (1990), a third of a 1980 cohort remained so after ten months. In the course of the process of grading and regrading an intense form of selection is at work leaving the less employable unemployed according to criteria that vary from country to country. The social and occupational characteristics of the stock of unemployed and of the the entrants are very different (Daniel, 1990). Of the EU countries Belgium, Ireland and Italy are the most seriously affected, with the unenviable record of between two-thirds and three-quarters of all unemployed having been so for more than a year. At the other end of the scale, the United Kingdom (41 per cent) and France (44 per cent) are the least affected. In between come Portugal (48 per cent), Federal Germany (49 per cent), the Netherlands (50 per cent) and Spain (59 per cent).[3]

By 1975, the proportions of unemployed in Western Europe out of work for more than a year (12 per cent to 34 per cent) were already considerably higher than those in Canada, the USA and Sweden (1.3 per cent to 6.2 per cent). Between 1975 and 1979, long-term unemployment worsened dramatically and to a much greater extent than overall unemployment, its share virtually doubling within the EC (see Figure IA.1 in Appendix). After 1979 the growth of long-term unemployment slowed. Between 1983 and 1989 unemployment rates began to drop somewhat, yet with some exceptions long-term unemployment did not follow suit, indeed from 1986 to 1989 its proportion continued to increase everywhere except in the UK, France and the Netherlands where it fell, and in Federal Germany where it remained stable. On the other hand, in the remaining OECD countries, long-term unemployment gave ground in 1989 as did overall unemployment.

The most incongruous feature of a peculiarly European manifestation is that in some countries it exists alongside a labour shortage. This Introduction will offer various explanations or interpretations of long-term unemployment, at the same time referring to specific chapters of the book for more detailed examination.

A 'congested' labour market?

Implicit or explicit there is a tendency to explain the longer duration of unemployment in terms of the level of overall employment: the greater the numbers of unemployed, the harder it is to get back to work and the longer the waiting stretch. In effect, on the evidence, EU countries have simultaneously high levels of unemployment and substantial proportions of unemployed of more than a year's standing, the degrees may vary but are comparable. The assumption is tenable only if outflows are less considerable than inflows, if job creation is insufficient to satisfy demand, as seems to be the case in Europe.

The opposite assumption appears to be equally plausible: the high level of unemployment in EU countries is to be explained by the existence of a stock of unemployed built up over a period of years and of long or very long duration. The duration of unemployment also accounts for the high level of overall unemployment. Layard *et al.* (1991) have refined the analysis by comparing inflows into unemployment and the length of unemployment.[4] They divide OECD countries into three groups. The first consisting of countries where there are few inflows into unemployment but many long-term unemployed (EU countries); the second group showing few inflows into unemployment and slight long-term unemployment (Scandanavian countries); the third being characterised by numerous inflows into unemployment and very little long-term unemployment (USA, Canada and Australia). There is then no simple, direct correlation between inflows into unemployment and long-term unemployment.

Two countries, USA and Britain, are examples in this respect. In the USA the level of inflows and the median duration of unemployment are closely parallel. The slight lengthening of the duration of unemployment is linked to contingency variations in inflows and regresses with an

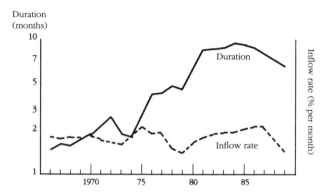

Figure I.1: Inflow rates and duration of unemployment
Britain, males 1962–1989

Source: Reproduced from Layard *et al* (1991:225)

improvement in employment. In Great Britain on the contrary – and its case doubtless holds for the rest of the European Union – the lengthening of unemployment from 1974 onwards is totally disconnected from the relatively slight variations in the inflows into unemployment. Figure I.1, taking men, provides a good illustration of this. Here it may be added that in 1989 Belgium affords the highly improbable instance of the best short-term unemployment rate and the highest long-term unemployment; Canada affords the contrary pattern with the worst rate of short-term unemployment and one of the lowest proportions of long-term unemployed. But there is no evident correlation between these two extremes.[5]

The congestion of the labour market serves to make it difficult to find an exit from unemployment; the number of jobs available being insufficient to satisfy the demands of the unemployed is advanced as the cause of this congestion and waiting-time (Salais, 1980). But if such were the case long-term unemployment would only rise substantially if the latest inflows provided the first outflows: in a well-ordered waiting-line on the contrary, long-term unemployment would increase only gradually in accordance with disparities between inflows and outflows. The question then arises as to whether there is greater congestion in Europe than in other OECD countries. Very probably there is, but measuring and comparing the level of congestion at the outflow from unemployment country by country is a complex operation involving at once the increase in population of working age and rates of activity (themselves variable according to the employment situation), the number of jobs created and the number lost,[6] hence to some degree the level of economic growth and the mobility of the labour market (lack of mobility in employment or high labour force turnover).

Between 1979 and 1989 economic growth (measured by GDP) was lower in the EC than in the rest of the OECD as was growth in employment:[7] average annual increase in the number of jobs occupied was 0.4 for the EC and 1.1 for the OECD taken together including the EC. In Europe of the Community the increase was brought about by substituting more labour-intensive capital; productivity was further improved than elsewhere. Would this imply that the European countries went further in replacing manual or unskilled workers by machines requiring more highly skilled operation, and so account for these lower grades being excluded from employment and their substantial presence in overall and long-term unemployment?

In fact there is no strict correlation between growth in productivity, long-term unemployment and shedding of manual and unskilled workers. In Britain, Ireland, the USA and perhaps in France there is indeed a high proportion of manual or unskilled workers in long-term unemployment, whereas between 1979 and 1989 growth in productivity was considerably higher in France than in Britain. In Italy and Spain the exclusion of manual workers does not appear as a factor, even so growth in productivity was markedly higher. In the USA manual workers were clearly casualties of unemployment, at the same time growth in productivity was very slight.

Exiting from unemployment appears to be difficult insofar as workers have little mobility in the labour market. Incumbent workers ('insiders') evidently cling to their jobs with the connivance of their employers, all the more so given the high level of unemployment. High labour turnover serves to allow those out of work to enter or re-enter jobs vacated so long as they have the right skills; it increases the probability of exchanges between employment and unemployment and may reduce the length of waiting in unemployment. But the high degree of stability in the labour market, for life almost, makes the business of placing job-seekers chancy and difficult. Likewise, significant cross-regional or cross-zonal labour mobility enables the effects of territorial differences in unemployment levels to be reduced, provided job-seekers move into areas where the employment situation is more favourable.

OECD data, available only for some countries and for earlier years, tend to show that within the EC these two forms of mobility are weaker than elsewhere,[8] confirming in part at least the assumption made. In Europe of the Community the rate of turnover in the labour force fell throughout the 1970s and at the start of the 1980s in every country, while remaining very high in the USA and in Finland; though high at first in Britain, it weakened significantly between 1971 and 1984 when unemployment and long-term unemployment showed a considerable increase; turnover is lowest in France and Italy, figures being closely comparable with those in Britain. Residential mobility is high only in the USA, Sweden and Norway, countries where long-term unemployment is low; everywhere else it is low, even in countries where long-term unemployment is virtually non-existent. Furthermore, account needs to be taken of regional divisions, where factors of size and population density can have an impact on the measure of mobility. A move away implies economic, social and human costs which are all the higher in the case of a depressed region. In conditions of unemployment, support within the family circle and the nexus of social relationships is beyond price. Europe with its long history is perhaps more responsive to the warmth of affection and friendship.

A deregulated labour market?

In classical economic theory, the regulation of the property market along with that of the labour market is carried out automatically by an invisible hand (i.e. via the mechanism of prices and wages). When unemployment rises, the price of labour ought ideally to drop given the competitive pressure of job-seekers, so bringing about a resumption of job availability and a fall-off in unemployment until an irreducible equilibrium point is reached. In this model there is no place at all for long-term unemployment. But since the 1973 oil shock, facts no longer accord with theory and economists are puzzled. Indeed, with unemployment rates as high as they are in Europe (due to long-term unemployment), the price of labour should have dropped not just in face value but in real terms, so leading to a recovery of employment. Instead, such a drop has not occurred or has been too slight in most European countries. So why has there been wage rigidity combined with a high rate of unemployment, at a level that appears intractable, preventing a return to equilibrium?

A primary reason for this rigidity, put forward by free market economists, is that when governments accord compensatory unemployment benefits that are sufficiently high or long-lasting, these act as a disincentive on those who receive them. With the unemployed no longer fulfilling their role in seeking to compete in the labour market, a severe shortage of labour should ensue, an increase in wage levels and a further thrust in unemployment likely to be self-perpetuating given the level of benefits. In fact, none of the more serious attempts made to show, instance by instance, the impact of unemployment benefit on the level of unemployment, and on that of long-term unemployment in particular, has produced no more than partial and limited results. In France, for example, longitudinal data have evinced that the impact is restricted to those receiving very high compensation (paid out before entering unemployment). As regards the rest, the majority of unemployed, unemployment benefit has little appreciable effect on the return to work (Florens *et al.*, 1990; Joutard and Werquin, 1990).

The complexity and diversity of the regulations that lay down the conditions for receiving such benefit, the level and duration of payment, make comparisons tricky and difficult. OECD gives typical examples, such as that of an average manual worker in his prime, with given family circumstances and having worked long enough to be allowed access to maximum benefit, but without taking into account supplementary allowances such as housing benefit (in Great Britain, in particular). However the OECD table is interpreted, there is no apparent overall correlation between the level and/or duration of unemployment benefit and the rate of long-term unemployment. It is true that in an analysis of the influence of several institutional variables on the level of unemployment (Layard *et al.*, 1991), the duration and level of benefit appear to have a significant impact on variations in the level of unemployment from one country to another (length of payment periods combined); but the duration of unemployment, more particularly, eludes these attempts at explanation.

On the basis of three family models of average manual workers of prime age, OECD[9] has calculated replacement rates for lost wages and the duration for payment of insurance allowances (not including welfare benefit) without revealing a clear correlation across the member countries of the Organisation (see Appendix Table IA.2). In Britain, the rate of replacement is much lower than in other EEC countries – a fixed sum, though payment is for an unlimited period. This appears to lead to very substantial proportions of long-term, and especially very long-term unemployment, with the unemployed making do with their benefit. But this is open to doubt, because in Sweden, Finland and Norway, benefit rates are far higher, payment lasts from 60 days up to two years and compensation varies from 90 per cent to 59 per cent. Nevertheless, unemployment in these countries is low and long-term unemployment barely exists.

Another OECD survey, which Michael White (Chapter 1) draws on, shows how wage rigidity occurs when wages no longer follow variations in the unemployment rate, whether short-term or long-term. This rigidity, which is measured for OECD countries, is clearly correlated with the increase in unemployment between 1973 and 1987[10]. One group of countries – the Netherlands, Britain, France and Germany – provide simultaneous evidence of both marked rigidity and a marked increase in unemployment. However, the proportion of long-term unemployment varies between 41 per cent and 49 per cent, which is more or less average for the EU. On the other hand, low rigidity and an insignificant increase in unemployment are to be found in Sweden, Canada and the USA, which are also the countries with the least significant long-term unemployment levels. It has to be recognised that there is no certain correlation here. Belgium is an exception in having average rigidity, a significant increase in unemployment and a particularly high proportion of long-term unemployed. Wage rigidity may account for the overall level of unemployment, but it is much less effective in explaining long-term unemployment.

In any case, this rigidity itself surely requires explanation. How does it come about? At this point one needs to turn to macroeconomic or macrosociological studies that look into national institutions and how they function, conventions and regulations, in short, relations based on power and social compromise between one class and another.

In the case of Britain, Michael White (Chapter 1) points out that in spite of unemployment wages have continued to rise markedly, particularly in the major manufacturing industries. The British system of wage-fixing is decentralised and fragmented. The government is not empowered to intervene and impose its will, nor even recommend an incomes or employment policy; employers are not grouped in national associations for the purposes of wage-fixing; and unions, weakened by the recession and Mrs Thatcher's policies, are divided. For these reasons, wage negotiations are most frequently carried out establishment by establishment, as close as possible to the work force. Such a system, virtually a freely competitive market, should entail a lowering of wages. However, management in the major British industries seems inclined to satisfy wage demands in return for workers accepting an increase in productivity and rationalisation, an intensification of productive processes and a substitution of capital for labour. Such a compromise leads unions themselves to contribute to reductions in manpower, to increasing unemployment and indirectly to long-term unemployment.

In West Germany (Jacobi and Müller-Jentsch, 1990), unions and management are implicitly agreed not to block technological modernisation of the productive apparatus, thereby safeguarding the country's international competitiveness, which contributes to the maintenance of employment. The whole country is geared towards exports. Instead of fighting in support of wage demands or job security (having in mind that cross-enterprise mobility is higher than elsewhere in the EU), the unions have directed their efforts at working hours with tangible results such as a 35-hour week in several branches. They have further agreed to greater flexibility in hours and not insignificant reductions in wages. In fact, real wages fell between 1980 and 1985 before rising again in 1986 and 1987. For their part and with financial support from the government, employers have set up schemes whereby those unemployed who lack skills can develop them in line with the requirements of modernisation. This so-called 'Skills Offensive' (Chapter 3) has not had the expected results. Doubtless, a compromise of this nature offers an explanation for the unemployment rate having remained considerably lower than it is in Great Britain, even if the place occupied by long-term unemployment is somewhat larger (49 per cent as compared with 41 per cent).

In both countries there is little intervention by central government. Negotiations between unions and management play a very large role, but with contrasting results. Wage levels so negotiated have evident repercussions on the level of unemployment. Any increase in wages makes job vacancies more costly and may lead to redundancies, and vice versa.

Is economic policy responsible for unemployment?

Government intervention in relation to the level of unemployment is exercised through the major devices for equilibrium in the economy and budgetary and monetary policy. Over the last ten years most European countries have opted – more or less energetically and more or less consistently – for budgetary rigour so as to ensure the stability of their currency within Europe and to reduce inflation and the wage/inflation spiral, all with a view to ensuring that they are competitive in international markets. Such national decisions on economic policy are held to be responsible for the size of unemployment in these countries. The question is how these options can be modified so as to ease the burden of unemployment. The pressures brought about by the internationalisation of markets and more recently by the ties of interdependence within the European Union appear insurmountable (International Economic Policy Group of *L'Observatoire française des conjonctures économiques*, OFCE, 1992; Solow, 1991). The few experiences of boosting the economy and relaxing stringency (Socialist government in France, 1981–3; Mrs Thatcher in Britain in 1987) were scarcely convincing, being followed inexorably by rising inflation, a reduced share in the export markets and finally worsening unemployment. Nor is it certain that a shift in macroeconomic policy would lead to a drop in unemployment. If the level of inflows into unemployment is not abnormally high, it is a case above all of finding the means of reducing long-term unemployment. It is by no means certain that those who have been unemployed for a year or longer would find a ready exit if the economy recovered. The experience of recent years in countries where long-term unemployment affects mainly unskilled workers (chiefly Britain, France and Federal Germany) provides confirmation of this. Labour shortages have appeared in parallel with a continuing high level of long-term unemployment. The unemployed are not all equal in value. The longer the time spent unemployed the less employable they become in the eyes of employers; further, harsh selection procedures operate in the course of job search.

The options open for exercising the major devices for equilibrium in the national economy, implying as they do specific decisions as to a desirable or acceptable volume of unemployment, are political options. It happens that they are applied outside any form of public debate since they are too technical. According to Korpi (1991), in order for governments to be induced to pursue a vigorous full-employment policy, three conditions are needed: (1) the problem of unemployment should receive open and public debate; (2) the means of implementing such a policy should be available and familiar to the public; (3) the possibility of a change of government should be generally recognised. If these conditions are met, full employment can be as much an objective of the right as of the left, since electoral pressures decide the priorities. One should see the possible effects of political action on the turning points of the waves of unemployment. The two long waves of unemployment in the 1930s and the years 1975–80 were separated by an unprecedented period of full employment. In comparing 18 OECD countries, Korpi (1991: 331, Table 3) observes that the stronger the left is, the lower the level of unemployment; however imperfect this correlation, it is yet much sounder than that between unemployment and economic indicators such as growth and inflation. Exceptions are Japan, Switzerland and Germany. The countries of the EC almost all find themselves, during the phase of low unemployment, in a median position as regards the strength of the left and the level of unemployment.

In regard to the recent period (1973–86), characterised by an upsurge in unemployment and a weakening of the position of wage earners in conflicts, Korpi further points to modes of settling conflicts. In centralised tripartite negotiation, government, management and unions take account of each other's interests; the model is typical of countries where the left is strong and has been in power for a considerable time, unemployment increasing only slightly.

The pluralistic model in which parties to the conflict are antagonistic and do not search for a compromise that takes account of the others' interests is characteristic of countries where the left is weak. The countries where pluralism obtains, in particular those in the EC, witnessed the highest growth in unemployment between 1972 and 1973 and 1985 and 1986. However, the exceptions are too numerous for the pattern to carry conviction. New Zealand, Australia, Italy, Canada and the USA register low rates of increase in unemployment in spite of their pluralism and the moderate or poor showing of the left in these countries.

The political measures in favour of employment implemented by governments in different countries and the funds earmarked for it without doubt have a more direct effect on the number of unemployed, long-term unemployment and the socio-demographic characteristics of the unemployed (see Appendix, Table IA.3). OECD has thrown light on the essential role of national employment agencies. The number of unemployed per agency official bears a close relation to the rate of long-term unemployment. In Sweden there are 9 unemployed to each official and a rate of long-term unemployment of 0.1 per cent; in France, 78 unemployed to each official and a rate of 3.5 per cent. One can express reserves as to the basis for this accounting but the tendency is beyond dispute. A well-staffed agency is able to spare time to make personal contacts with those who are unemployed, help them to find their bearings and advise them on jobs available.

The sums assigned to employment by each country as a proportion of GDP confirm the major role that an active and well funded policy has in regard to overall rates of unemployment (see Appendix Table IA.3); but as regards long-term unemployment financing is less effective. An employment service that is comprehensively funded and motivated hastens the integration or reintegration of the easier cases, thus gaining a few weeks or months on the stock of those who have been unemployed for under a year, but it appears to have no effect on those who have been unemployed for longer, except naturally in Sweden.

The development in effectiveness of the employment services in Sweden needs to be set against a restrictive measure: refusal of the third offer of employment entails the withdrawal of benefit. Such a measure has never, at least for the time being, met with acceptance in the EU countries. Solow (1991: 31) has stressed this 'Euro-sclerosis' (i.e. the notion that consists in believing that the unemployed cannot be required to fill jobs that are essential to society). Perhaps there are signs here of more extreme individualism. Policies in regard to employment certainly reflect not merely political intentions as they emerge from the balance of forces opposing one another, but a whole system of social norms and representations as well, which has taken shape over the years in the conduct of social relations.

The huge diversity in the long-term unemployed

Governments set up programmes to further employment for this or that category of workers and to curb the growth of the labour force. While shifting unemployment on to other categories, the effect of these measures is generally deemed positive (Cornilleau *et al.*, 1990; Bourdet and Persson, 1991). In virtually all OECD countries there is a hard core of the labour force – males between 25 and 49 – that is in general less affected by unemployment, including long-term unemployment. Alongside this hard core the other age/sex/skill groups show unemployment rates that are very varied and of greater or lesser duration according to the country. National models appear to be rooted in 'national forms of societal organisation' (Iribarne, 1990a) (see Appendix, Tables IA.4a and IA.4b).

In Great Britain men more frequently face unemployment, including long-term unemployment, than women; in France the contrary occurs. Ireland is the only other European country to follow the British pattern. In Spain (Chapter 5) women who have already had a job, been made redundant or stopped work on the birth of children, form the main body of unemployed, including long-term unemployed. In this capacity they have replaced girls looking for their first job.

The same goes for those who are older, over 50 or 55. Their part in unemployment is unexpectedly high, especially so in long-term unemployment. It is highest in France, for men as for women, and lowest in Germany. Yet in both there have been specific measures to increase early retirement. In France 60 is now the age of retirement, even so rates of activity have dropped dramatically from 50 onwards (sole instance for OECD). In spite of this, long-term unemployment has barely eased. This policy is based on consensus between government, unions and management. For the one side, it offers a well earned rest; for the other, an opportunity to shed employees who are difficult and less adaptable to new technology. In Germany retirement has remained at 65, rates of activity are substantially the same, and benefit is scheduled in case of unemployment in anticipation of early retirement after 60. But there has not been, as there has in France, a massive consensus for excluding older age groups.

The concentration of unemployment on manual workers is particularly significant in Great Britain and Ireland, somewhat so in France, but much less in Federal Germany and still less so in Spain (Layard *et al.*, 1991). In France the unemployed include a considerable number of unskilled workers (Chapter 2). In countries that took on board time-and-motion models of production, in which tasks are fragmented as far as they can be and divested of any intelligence and autonomy, manual and unskilled categories appear to have been replaced by robots. These too are countries where long-term unemployment is heavily concentrated in categories that are ostracised socially speaking. Here again, across the systematic rejection of those who are most disadvantaged that, in very different degrees, characterises European societies, manifold social forces which are historically entrenched come into play.

The opportunities available for young people on the labour market varies a great deal from country to country. In France, Federal Germany, Great Britain and the Netherlands, unemployment among youths and their part in long-term unemployment is moderate. In Italy, Spain and Ireland high figures occur in spite of measures consistently applied to make access to employment easier. Here training schemes may provide an insight. In Federal Germany where dual schemes for vocational training (schools and firms), administered by employers and unions, have been very fruitful, unemployment among young people is very slight with very little long-term unemployment. Over ten years the burden of unemployment has swung away from young people to the older categories (Chapter 3). In Britain where the training scheme system has broken down, the proportion of young people is high, as it is in France where little is done for those at the bottom of the class to prepare them for a job and where employers are mistrustful of forms of training that do not provide formal qualifications. In Italy (Chapter 4), the rapid increase in the school population during the last fifteen years, the laxity which has prevailed in the matter of selection procedures and the awarding of qualifications, and an ideology hostile to capitalism and industry widespread among young people have acted against their being taken on. Employers prefer candidates who have already acquired experience in industry, and this accounts for the absence of unemployment among men over 25. Young people refuse to acknowledge the loss in value of qualifications and prefer to wait for an opening that corresponds with their level of ability; close-knit family life enables them to do so. A collection of social forces act as systematic regulators of access into the labour market, and it will take a long time for their effect to be modified.

Conclusion

This outline of the forms and structure of long-term unemployment as it varies between countries shows that as a problem it is both related to and distinct from short-term unemployment; the one is not simply an extension of the other and this needs to be borne in mind when studying the question. For various reasons the long-term unemployed seem to have lost their competitive role in the labour market, and for them re-entry is very difficult. Furthermore, we have sought to provide evidence that the social constituents in long-term unemployment vary greatly: perhaps it is susceptible to analysis *en bloc* by being made up of similar, undifferentiated elements. Examination of the various causes of long-term unemployment advanced by researchers in different fields and establishments leaves one largely dissatisfied, probably because the distinction between long- and short-term unemployment, the degree to which the former is unrelated, has not been recognised. Moreover, taking indicators piecemeal and studying how they relate to the problem of unemployment as a whole is bound to result in failure. Even resorting to more sophisticated forms of statistical analysis has not produced more satisfying results. Divide the difficulty, said Descartes, in other words study the different elements of unemployment separately.

The proposition to analyse long-term unemployment, or rather its different manifestations, as the expression and consequence of multiple social forces rooted in the history of social relations and customs offers a more promising direction, even if its findings so far fail to carry conviction. Yet however promising, the line of approach is long, drawn out and tortuous: to analyse 'societal cohesion', the manner in which each society functions as a system, involves the preparation of monographs at national or regional levels (as in Italy) in order to discover how the various elements identified in this Introduction interrelate. Political institutions, forms of wage negotiation, practices in regard to the division of labour, systems of training, role and degree of presence of government and class divisions all need to be analysed and related so as to arrive at an understanding of the tenacity of long-term unemployment for each country. Subsequently such monographs will require collating so that interpretations can be put to the test and lead to results that have general application. We hope this book will give rise to this type of team collaboration.

Notes

1. Cf Tables 1a, 1b, 1c and Figure 1 in Statistical Appendix.
2. Labour force includes both those with jobs and those in job search.
3. Cf Tables 1a, 1b, 1c and Figure 1 in Statistical Appendix.
4. Layar *et al.*, 1991.
5. Cf Tables 1b and 1c in Statistical Appendix.
6. Cf Figure 3 in Appendix for state of labour market (changes in available labour force, employment and unemployment) by sex in respect of countries treated here.
7. OECD, 1991, *Employment Outlook*, 37, 39.
8. Cf OECD, 1991, *Employment Outlook*, 56, Tables 2.13, 2.14.
9. Cf OECD, 1991, *Employment Outlook*, 222–8, 256–7.
10. OECD, 1989, *Economies in Transition*, Chapter 1, Figure p.51.

STATISTICAL APPENDIX TO INTRODUCTION

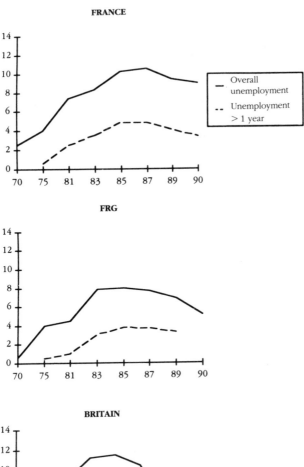

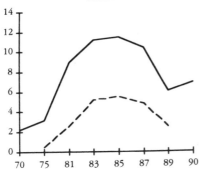

Figure IA.1 Unemployment in terms of duration
(as % of total labour force)

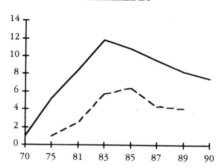

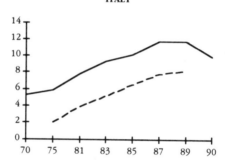

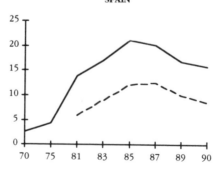

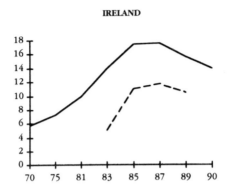

IRELAND

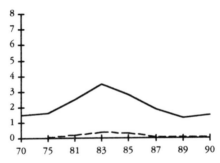

SWEDEN

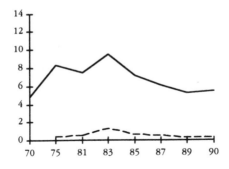

UNITED STATES

Source: OECD, 1991, *Employment Outlook,* July

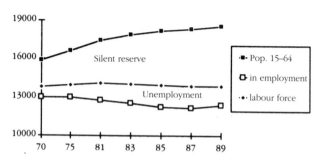

FRANCE males

Silent reserve

Unemployment

Pop. 15–64
in employment
labour force

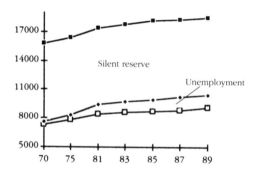

FRANCE Females

Silent reserve

Unemployment

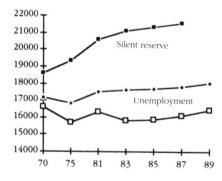

FRG Males

Silent reserve

Unemployment

Figure IA.2
State of labour market by gender (thous.)

FRG Females

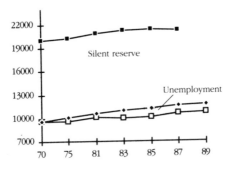

UNITED KINGDOM Males

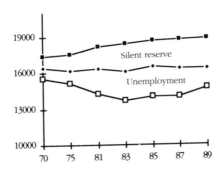

UNITED KINGDOM Females

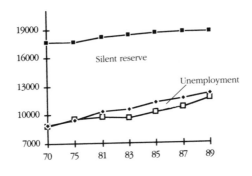

ITALY Males

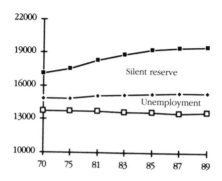

ITALY Females

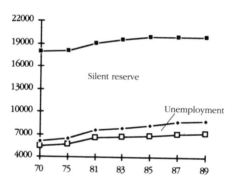

IRELAND Males

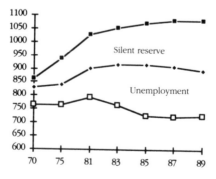

IRELAND Females

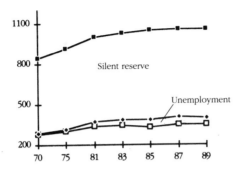

NETHERLANDS Males

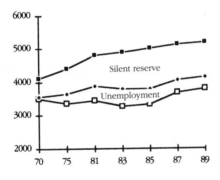

NETHERLANDS Females

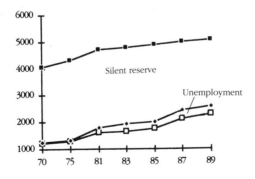

Table IA.1a
Overall unemployment rate (as % of total labour force)

COUNTRY	1970	1975	1979	1981	1983	1985	1986	1987	1988	1989	1990
France	2,5	4,0	5,9	7,4	8,3	10,2	10,4	10,5,	10,0	9,4	9,0
FRG	0,6	4,0	3,3	4,5	7,9	8,0	7,6	7,6	7,6	6,8	5,1
United Kingdom	2,2	3,2	4,6	9,0	11,2	11,5	11,6	10,4	8,3	6,1	6,9
Netherlands	1,0	5,2	5,4	8,5	11,8	10,9	10,3	9,6	9,2	8,3	7,5
Italy	5,3	5,8	7,6	7,8	9,3	10,1	10,9	11,8	11,8	11,8	9,9
Spain	2,5	4,3	8,4	13,8	17,0	21,1	20,8	20,1	19,1	16,9	15,9
Ireland	5,8	7,3	7,1	9,9	14,0	17,4	17,4	17,6	16,7	15,6	14,0
Belgium	1,9	4,5	7,5	10,2	13,2	12,3	11,6	11,3	10,3	9,3	7,9
Sweden	1,5	1,6	2,1	2,5	3,5	2,8	2,7	1,9	1,6	1,3	1,5
Norway	0,8	2,3	2,0	2,0	3,4	2,6	2,0	2,1	3,2	4,9	5,2
Finland	1,9	2,2	5,9	4,8	5,4	5,0	5,3	5,0	4,5	3,4	3,4
Australia	1,6	4,8	6,1	5,7	9,8	8,1	8,0	8,0	7,1	6,1	6,9
Canada	5,6	6,9	7,4	7,5	11,8	10,4	9,5	8,8	7,7	7,5	8,1
USA	4,8	8,3	5,8	7,5	9,5	7,1	6,9	6,1	5,4	5,2	5,4
Japan	1,1	1,9	2,1	2,2	2,6	2,6	2,8	2,8	2,5	2,3	2,1

Sources: OECD, 1991, *Labour force statistics 1969–1989;* Eurostat 1988, *Long-term Unemployment*

Table IA.1b
Long-term unemployment rate (as % of total labour force)

COUNTRY	1975	1979	1981	1983	1985	1986	1987	1988	1989	1990
France	0,6	1,8	2,5	3,5	4,8	5,0	4,8	4,5	4,1	3,4
FRG	0,5	0,9	1,0	3,1	3,8	3,7	3,7	3,5	3,3	-
United Kingdom	0,5	1,4	2,6	5,2	5,5	5,2	4,8	3,7	2,5	-
Netherlands	1,0	1,9	2,5	5,8	6,4	6,1	4,4	4,6	4,1	-
Italy	2,0	3,9	3,9	5,2	6,6	7,2	7,8	8,1	8,3	-
Spain	-	2,3	6,0	9,1	12,2	11,8	12,5	11,7	9,9	8,6
Ireland	1,4	2,7	-	5,1	11,1	11,2	11,7	11,0	10,5	-
Belgium	1,3	4,6	-	8,7	8,5	8,1	8,5	8,0	7,1	-
Sweden	0,1	0,1	0,2	0,4	0,3	0,2	0,1	0,1	0,1	0,1
Norway	-	0,1	0,1	0,2	0,2	0,1	0,1	0,2	0,6	1,0
Finland	-	-	-	1,1	-	0,9	1,0	-	0,2	-
Australia	-	1,1	1,2	2,7	2,5	2,2	2,3	1,6	1,4	1,5
Canada	0,1	0,3	0,3	0,6	1,1	1,0	0,8	0,6	0,5	0,5
USA	0,4	0,2	0,5	1,3	0,7	0,6	0,5	0,4	0,3	0,3
Japan	-	-	-	0,3	-	0,5	0,6	0,5	0,4	0,4

Sources: OECD, 1991, *Labour force statistics 1969–1989*; Eurostat, 1988, *Long-term Unemployment*

Table IA.1c
Percentage of long-term unemployed in overall unemployment

COUNTRY	1975	1979	1981	1983	1985	1986	1987	1988	1989	1990
France	16,3	31,0	33,4	42,5	46,8	47,8	45,5	44,8	43,9	37,8
FRG	11,8	28,7	22,4	39,3	47,9	48,9	48,2	46,7	49,0	-
United Kingdom	14,8	29,5	29,3	46,6	48,1	45,0	45,9	44,7	40,8	-
Netherlands	18,6	35,9	29,6	49,4	58,7	59,5	46,2	50,0	49,9	-
Italy	33,8	51,2	50,3	56,3	65,7	66,1	66,4	69,0	70,4	-
Spain	-	27,5	43,6	53,6	57,8	56,6	62,0	61,5	58,5	54,0
Ireland	19,1	38,2	-	36,4	63,8	64,5	66,4	66,0	67,3	-
Belgium	29,7	61,6	-	65,8	69,2	70,3	74,9	77,5	76,3	-
Sweden	6,2	6,8	6,0	10,3	11,4	8,0	8,0	8,2	6,5	4,8
Norway	-	3,8	3,0	6,7	8,3	6,7	5,0	6,3	11,6	19,2
Finland	-	-	-	19,8	-	6,0	19,0	-	6,9	-
Australia	-	18,1	21,1	27,5	30,9	27,5	28,6	23,0	23,0	21,6
Canada	1,3	3,5	4,2	4,8	10,3	10,9	9,4	7,4	6,8	5,7
USA	5,3	4,2	6,7	13,3	9,5	8,7	8,1	7,4	5,7	5,6
Japan	-	-	-	12,9	-	17,2	20,2	20,2	18,7	19,1

Sources: OECD, 1991, Labour force statistics 1969–1989; Eurostat 1988, Long-term Unemployment

Table IA.2
Replacement rate of wage of average manual worker by duration of
unemployment

	Span of continuous employment, per year								1988		
	Single				Married, dependent partner				Unemployment rate	Long-term unemployment rate	Proportion of L-TU in overall unemployment
	Year				Year						
	1	2	3	4	1	2	3	4			
France	59	42	27	26	59	44	32	32	10,0	4,5	44,5
Germany	58	52	52	52	58	52	52	52	7,6	3,5	46,7
United Kingdom	16	16	16	16	26	26	26	26	8,3	3,7	44,7
Netherlands	70	70	40	40	70	70	58	58	9,2	4,6	50,0
Spain	62	60	0	0	75	60	27	14	19,1	11,7	61,5
Ireland	29	23	20	20	43	36	34	34	16,7	11,0	66,0
Sweden	90	37	27	27	90	44	36	36	1,6	0,1	8,2
USA	25	0	0	0	25	0	0	0	5,4	0,4	7,4

* Hypothetical replacement rate, expressed as % of gross earnings of average manual worker in 1988 (in case of Germany, percentage of earnings after tax) excluding other benefits.

Source: OECD, 1991, Employment Outlook

Table IA.3
Public expenditure assigned to labour market programmes
(expressed as % of GDP in 1989)

	France	Germany	UK*	Netherlands	Italy**	Spain	Ireland	Sweden	USA
Admin. and employment services	0,12	0,22	0,14	0,08	0,08	0,12	0,17	0,21	0,07
Training schemes	0,32	0,33	0,24	0,22	0,03	0,10	0,50	0,44	0,10
Provision for young people	0,20	0,05	0,22	0,07	0,69	0,08	0,38	0,05	0,03
Assistance with placement	0,04	0,19	0,03	0,05	-	0,50	0,22	0,13	0,01
Provision for the handicapped	0,05	0,23	0,02	0,66	-	0,17	0,73	0,04	0,04
Unemployment	1,27	1,2	0,84	2,42	0,40	2,33	2,95	0,55	0,47
Early retirement prompted by labour market conditions	0,65	0,02	-	-	0,32	0,09	-	0,09	-
TOTAL	2,65	2,25	1,50	3,50	1,52	3,21	4,39	2,20	0,73

* 1989–90 data   ** 1988 data

Table IA.4a

Unemployment rate (all durations) by age and sex – 1990

	Overall rate	< 25 years M	F	25–54 years M	F	> 55 years M	F
France	9,0	15,4	24,0	6,2	10,7	6,0	7,6
Germany*	5,1	7,2	9,0	5,5	8,5	8,3	11,9
UK	6,9	10,2	5,8	6,7	2,8	6,8	4,4
Netherlands	7,5	10,0	12,3	4,5	10,3	3,2	5,0
Italy**	9,9	25,8	37,8	4,4	12,0	1,7	2,2
Spain	15,9	26,2	39,7	9,3	20,6	8,4	7,2
Ireland***	14,0	24,6	19,4	16,8	7,2	15,2	8,2
Sweden	1,5	3,6	3,4	1,1	1,1	1,2	1,6
USA	5,4	10,8	10,5	4,4	4,5	3,8	2,8

* 1987
** age brackets are < 25 years, 25–59 years, > 60 years
*** 1989 figures

Table IA.4b

Proportion of L-TU (in overall unemployment) by age and sex – 1987

	< 25 years M	F	25–49 years M	F	> 50 years M	F
France	31,8	41,3	50,1	54,2	67,7	71,7
UK	37,4	26,2	59,4	31,5	63,0	53,9
Netherlands	26,3	26,5	62,1	48,7	71,7	54,5
Italy	64,3	70,2	64,5	67,0	51,8	54,6
Spain	58,7	70,6	61,6	73,5	64,2	71,5
Ireland	60,9	51,3	73,9	62,1	78,1	68,6

Source: Eurostat (SOEC), 1988, *Survey of Labour Forces, 1987 figures*

Table IA.5
Distribution of households by employment situation of partners

	Germany	France	United Kingdom	Italy	Netherlands	Ireland
COUPLES						
M and F working	18,3	26,9	27,5	23,7	15,8	11,3
M work, F unemp/non-wkg	20,4	18,6	17,7	40	27,3	34,5
M unemp/non-wkg, F wkg	1,9	3	1	1	1,8	2,1
M and F unemployed	0,2	0,3	0,5	0,01	0,2	1,0
M and F non-working	12,1	14,3	12,7	10	14,6	10,6
M and F unemp/non-wkg*	0,8	1,2	2,4	0,5	1,8	5,6
% of couples out of total number of households	53,7	64,3	63,7	75,2	61,5	65,1
HEAD OF HOUSEHOLD without partner (male or female)						
Working	19,6	15,6	12	12	15	12,4
Unemployed	2,1	1,5	1,9	0,5	2,9	2
Non-working	24,5	18,7	22,4	12,1	20,5	
TOTAL NUMBER (100) OF HOUSEHOLDS	24 358 200	20 575 800	21 455 700	15 613 400	5 418 800	997 800

* One unemployed, the other non-working

Source: Eurostat (SOEC) data, Labour Force Surveys, 1985, supplied by J.J.Sexton, Economic and Social Research Institute, Dublin

Table IA.6a
Unemployment rates for men depending on woman being employed
or unemployed

	Germany	France	UK	Italy	Nether-lands	Ireland
W empl.	2,4	3,2	3,1	0,3	2,9	9,4
W unempl.	11,3	10,8	17,0	0,3	11,6	32,6

Table IA.6b
Unemployment rates for women depending on man being employed
or unemployed

	Germany	France	UK	Italy	Nether-lands	Ireland
M empl.	7,2	9,0	7,8	7,5	8,3	15,8
M unempl.	28,5	26,6	35,0	9,1	28,1	46,3

Source: Compiled from Eurostat (SOEC) figure from labour force surveys 1985.
Supplied by J.J. Sexton, the Economic and Social Research Institute, Dublin

Table IA.7
Index of persistent unemployment with partner unemployed

MEN

	Germany	France	UK	Italy	Nether-lands	Ireland
W unempl. / W wking.	4,71	3,38	5,48	0	4,00	3,47

WOMEN

	Germany	France	UK	Italy	Nether-lands	Ireland
M unempl. / M wking.	3,96	2,96	4,49	1,21	3,39	2,93

By way of illustration, in France men are 3.38 times more often unemployed
when their partner is herself unemployed than when she is working.

CHAPTER 1

UNEMPLOYMENT AND EMPLOYMENT RELATIONS IN BRITAIN

Michael White

In Britain unemployment, especially long-term unemployment, is heavily concentrated among working-class occupations. It is widely experienced among manual workers, and also, though to a lesser extent, among those in the lower-paid and more routine non-manual jobs. It is little experienced in higher occupations or in intermediate occupations requiring technical or professional qualifications. So strong is this bias that it can be regarded as the single most conspicuous feature of how unemployment is distributed in Britain.

Why is unemployment concentrated in this way? Once the question is posed, answers may seem obvious. 'Unemployment affects people with little or no skill.' In fact, more skilled manual workers entered unemployment in the 1980s than any other group; coalminers, steelworkers, textile machine operators, and carpenters have all been heavily over-represented among Britain's long-term unemployed. 'Well then, it is because of the decline of certain industries.' Yet we do not find the managers, the accountants, or the technicians from those declining industries among the long-term unemployed. In a longer historical view, Britain has seen the virtual disappearance of two great classes of workers – farmworkers, and domestic servants – without either group creating a problem of long-term unemployment.

If we look at Britain's long-term unemployment as a whole, what is striking is how broadly based it is. Two thirds of long-term unemployed people have worked for large firms or in the public sector, one third have come from small firms. Manufacturing and service industries are represented roughly in proportion to employment. One quarter of long-term unemployed people have come directly from long-lasting jobs, and a similar proportion have held such jobs in the past before starting a downward slide; the remainder have come from relatively short-lived jobs. Although younger workers are over-represented, there are also many older workers, especially among those unemployed for two years or more. As already mentioned, there are many skilled workers as well as semi-skilled and unskilled. This breadth of unemployment makes its concentration within working-class occupations still more remarkable. In the 1980s, about 80 per cent of men in long-term unemployment came from a background in manual occupations, which provided about 45 per cent of the jobs for men at the time. Similarly, more than 90 per cent of women in long-term unemployment came from manual or routine non-manual occupations, which supplied about 60 per cent of the jobs for women.

Working-class unemployment in Britain is so big that, to explain it, one must virtually explain unemployment as a whole. It suggests that British unemployment may have grown out of the very same processes which have shaped the conditions under which manual workers are employed.

A similar thought occurred many years ago to William Beveridge, founder of the British Welfare State and, with John Maynard Keynes, of the 'full employment' policy of the post-war era. In the early 1900s, he observed that unemployment was concentrated among occupations, such as dock work or construction, where labour was hired casually by the hour.[1] This casual nature of employment, he reasoned, was also a large part of the explanation for unemployment. Casual employment indicated that the job market was poorly organized and chaotic, and could not respond efficiently to the pressures of economic change.

Of course, the situation of the 1980s or 1990s is far different from the situation of 1900. Casual employment has been reduced to a small part of the job market, and can no longer be thought to have much influence on unemployment. But the consequences of that historical tradition remain. It is no coincidence that in Britain manual workers are frequently referred to as hourly paid, a term which expresses both the calculative, monetary basis of the employment relationship, and its underlying fragility. These characteristics, as we shall try to show, have moulded the aims and actions of workers and their trade unions on one side, and of employers on the other. And from the interaction of the two sides has emerged the persistent mass unemployment of recent years.

What generates unemployment?

To explain why UK unemployment has been concentrated upon working-class occupations requires two steps. First, we need to outline what has generated the rising unemployment of the past two decades. Second, we need to describe the ways in which unemployment becomes allocated especially to people in manual and routine non-manual occupations. In reality, the two stages treated separately are not distinct but interwoven: the growth of unemployment and its concentration upon lower occupations are two aspects of the same process. At the end of the chapter, we will try to bring all together.

Wage rigidity

Economists have usually based their explanations of unemployment on wages, or more precisely, on some malfunctioning of the system of wage fixing. The classical economic theory, sometimes known as Say's Law, assumes that the supply of labour creates sufficient demand for its services by offering them at a wage just sufficiently low to be attractive to employers. Hence the labour market should balance or clear, leaving no unemployment. Implicitly, the mechanism that removes unemployment is, or should be, wage competition. But the labour market much of the time does not clear, and British economists were among the first to concern themselves with this awkward fact. For example, in the 1920s Alfred Pigou stressed that because many workers were reluctant to move to different areas in search of jobs, or lacked the skills to move into growth industries, effective wage competition was reduced.[2] Keynes, as a sideline to his theory of economic demand, developed the notion of 'wage stickiness', which was caused by the reluctance of workers to see existing wage differentials upset, and by employers' desire to avoid conflict.

With the rising British unemployment of the late 1960s and 1970s, the leading economic explanation was soon pointing towards the rising pressure of wage demands. These pressures were in turn generally seen as the result of the growing power of trade unions and the rising militancy of workers: a point which immediately connects with our focus upon working-class unemployment, since trade unions in Britain have largely been working-class institutions. By 1975, Samuel Brittan was influentially advocating monetarist economic policies to curb the inflation created by wage pressures, and reform of trade unions to remove or reduce their power over wages. These were among the chief policies pursued by the Thatcher government during the 1980s, but their consequences were not entirely as expected. Trade unions grew weaker, unemployment rose sharply, but wages continued to press relentlessly upward: in fact, they increased (in terms of real values) more rapidly than ever before. Were economists wrong, therefore, to stress the importance of wages and of trade unions? In our view, they were right to stress these factors, but wrong in their interpretation of how they operated.

To underline the importance of wages for British unemployment, one can turn to international comparisons. An analysis published by the OECD (1989) showed how changes in unemployment in each of 16 industrialised countries were related to wage rigidity in those same countries, over the period 1973 to 1987. An economy with high wage rigidity is one where wage increases continue regardless of the state of the job market, while an economy with high wage flexibility (evidently, the opposite of rigidity) is one where wage increases progress under boom conditions but become moderated or suppressed when there is a recession. The outcome of the OECD analysis is shown in Figure 1.1. It shows two rather distinct groups of countries, one with low wage rigidity and a low rate of increase of unemployment, the other with high wage rigidity and a high rate of increase of unemployment. The UK is at the extreme of the latter group, with an exceptionally high level of wage rigidity together with an exceptionally large increase in unemployment.

The importance of wage pressures for the UK can hardly be doubted, but the problem is to explain why these pressures should have continued both in a period when trade unions were strong and expanding (the late 1960s and much of the 1970s), and also in a period when trade unions were weak and contracting (the 1980s). It is hard to fit these facts to economists' notions of wage competition, since in a period of weak trade unions, such competition should be intensified and wage pressures accordingly should be reduced (the opposite of what the UK has apparently experienced). Economists therefore have had to invent a new set of forces to restrict competition in the 1980s, an endeavour in which they have so far convinced few people apart from themselves.[3]

Employers, unions and the state

An alternative way of approaching the issues is to examine society's arrangements for fixing wages and employment, the so-called institutions of the labour market. These include not only trade unions, but employers and the state. How far an economy in practice enforces wage flexibility or permits wage rigidity will depend largely on these social arrangements. During the 1980s, much research was carried out to compare the industrial countries in terms of their institutions, and this

MICHAEL WHITE

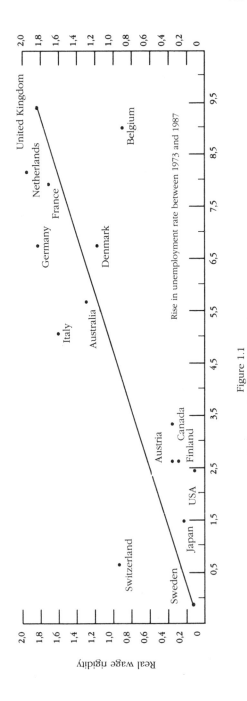

Figure 1.1
Real wage rigidity and unemployment

Source: OECD, 1989, Economies in Transition, diagram 2.6 (q.v. for further details and definitions)

work offers valuable insights for understanding the problems of the British labour market.[4]

In the first place, this research shows that there are other ways of achieving wage flexibility, and of keeping long-term unemployment at a low level, apart from having weak trade unions and a competitive free market. It is true that the USA, Canada and Switzerland, bastions of free enterprise with weak unions, have all been successful in controlling unemployment (see Figure 1.1). But equally successful have been Austria, Norway and Sweden, where trade unions are particularly strong, and where wages are fixed in a highly centralised way, at national level, with the state playing a leading part alongside unions and employers. It seems that what these otherwise contrasting groups of countries have in common is not the kind of system that they operate, but the consistency and cohesiveness of various aspects of that system. Countries where the systems are less consistent or coherent cannot be relied upon to restrain wages, foster employment, or generally to respond predictably to economic pressures. It will be correspondingly difficult for the government to guide such an inconsistent system towards any chosen objective.

By applying these ideas to Britain, we can begin to understand the sources of many of its problems. This is a country with a deep well-spring of inconsistencies: the land of individualism and the creator of modern industrial capitalism, but also with a welfare state the origins of which lie in the sixteenth century. It is not surprising that the institutions for wage fixing and employment have developed in a chaotic and self-contradictory manner, especially in the post-war period.

The legal framework in Britain is minimal, with an overriding belief in voluntary agreements between unions and employers. Unlike the Scandinavian countries, there is no central, national machinery for the regulation of wages. Neither the central union body, the TUC, nor the central employers' organisation, the CBI, has had an effective power base, and neither takes part in wage negotiations or has an influence on national employment policies. Yet, in the post-war period up to 1980, there was continual government intervention in wages, which was received with hostility by employers as well as unions.

Trade unions emerged early in the UK but developed in a fragmented manner, and with a degree of rivalry rather than mutual cooperation. Moreover, workers tended to be suspicious of central union leadership, and power has progressively moved to the local level, with shop stewards often having more influence over events than union officials. Similarly, large employers have tended to weaken their own industry bodies by their defections, and have actively promoted the decentralisation of wage agreements to the level of the workplace, which now dominates much of the UK system.

The overall tendency of the UK system of bargaining has therefore been centrifugal. Such a decentralised system, of course, makes it difficult for any government to promote the aim of wage flexibility, or to encourage employment as a priority. But this decentralised and fragmented situation should not be confused with a competitive labour market of the American type, where bargaining between trade unions and employers is unimportant for much of the economy. Britain's trade unions and leading employers are much too large and powerful for that to be possible. Trade union membership remains above 40 per cent nationally, despite a decade of erosion, and is particularly high in the public sector and in the large firm sector. Moreover, employment within the market sector of the economy is so highly concentrated in large companies that they enjoy great labour market power.

The resulting system revolves around the policies of the large employers and the leading trade unions in a way which is only weakly influenced by market forces or government policies. At one time unions may have the upper hand, at other times large employers. But both employers and unions know that they must live together in the long term: the other is too strong to be ignored, even when it is at its weakest. Furthermore, because the system is a decentralised one, decisions are made close to the workers and have to take account of worker reactions. The need to persuade workers has meant that their aspirations have been able to influence developments, whether these developments have been led by trade unions or by employers. But this apparently democratic feature of the decentralised British system has brought disadvantages to manual workers as well as advantages. Their own aspirations have cooperated in the growth of an unemployment of which they themselves, as a group, have been the chief victims.

Wages, unions and job loss

Workers' aspirations have, in fact, provided the linking theme of a period of twenty years, in which power has shifted between unions and employers, but always with wage rigidity dominant and unemployment becoming more entrenched.

The late 1960s, when employers were beginning to turn to policies of labour-saving investment, was also a period of rising expectations among lower-paid workers. Most workers at this period believed that affluence would rise progressively (Goldthorpe *et al*, 1968). Their unions were beginning to press, much more strongly than before, for higher wages. It was a time of increasing militancy (as elsewhere in Europe). At this time, manufacturing companies were moving towards the use of incentive payment systems on a large scale, and then towards productivity bargaining – the offer of wage increases to buy out inefficient working practices or to gain acceptance of new methods of working. In the face of union power, employers developed a reliance on various types of wage increases or financial incentives in order to achieve their aims with worker compliance. This may well have contributed to the rising inflation of the 1970s; by this time, unions had learned to build the expected rate of inflation into their next wage demand, and an explosive situation was developing.

But the 1970s did not turn out to be the decade of affluence that workers expected. By the second half of the 1970s, union power was beginning to decline. Monetarist economic policies were introduced by the Labour government in 1976 to curb inflation; unemployment was already rising steeply, but wage pressures – driven by disappointed aspirations – continued almost unabated. Leading employers were beginning to consider the possibility of new strategies in which the (at least passive) cooperation of the now weakened trade unions could be assumed. At the end of the 1970s, with the advent of the Thatcher decade, government took up an anti-union stance for the first time since the war.

The weakening of trade unions, coupled with the further doubling of unemployment in 1980–81 (focused, as we have seen, largely upon manual workers) might have been expected to lead to a reduction of wage pressures. The actual outcome was quite different. Between 1980 and 1988, the cost of living in Britain rose by 54 per cent but average wages rose by 95 per cent. The rate of wage increase, more than four per cent per annum in real terms, is the highest ever recorded over such a long period in Britain. And unemployment continued at an extremely high level through five years of uninterrupted economic growth after the recession.

There appears to be only one reasonable explanation for the high wage increases of the 1980s, when coupled with weakened trade unions and high unemployment. Employers (or at least those employers that were in a position to lead) chose or preferred a high rate of wage increase. They did so because they were at the same time intensifying their policies of rationalisation and workforce reductions (Ingram, 1991; White, 1991). Through a positive policy of raising wages, they could gain the acceptance of trade unions and the compliance of the majority of workers – conditions to which, as stressed earlier, the British system makes them sensitive. Because of the large increase in productivity that they were able to achieve in this period, leading employers were able to offer substantial increases in earnings yet still emerge with increased profits. The combination of workforce reductions with high wage increases not only aggravated unemployment, but ensured that it became a persistent and intractable problem.

From this historical train of events, we can identify some reasons to explain why mass unemployment has been focused particularly upon manual workers. Through trade union organisation, manual workers can press for a higher standard of living, and this they began to do in the 1960s as aspirations generally advanced. But in doing so, they aroused employers' interest in making productivity gains and in seeking rationalization of the labour force. Manual workers themselves were, and are, the primary target for such changes. In part, this is because of the different nature of the tasks carried out by manual and white-collar workers. Manual work, organised along the lines of narrow tasks often closely interdependent with machines, is much more easily altered by new technology and new systems of working. Further, in the previous decades when manual workers were chiefly interested in job security, many customs and working practices had grown up to maintain the number of jobs and to restrict the scope of management in rationalising jobs. As workers and unions changed their priorities, employers had scope to bargain for removal of these restrictive practices, leading to reductions in the numbers of workers employed, in return for wage increases.

In pressing for a higher standard of living, therefore, manual workers made themselves vulnerable to rationalisation and eventually to mass unemployment. Moreover, the trade unions, which were the instrument of worker power in pursuing a better life, were also of great help to employers, at a later stage, in organising and legitimating the reduction of the workforce. Recent research in Britain has, indeed, demonstrated that the greater the presence of unions in a firm, the greater the reduction of employment there during the first part of the 1980s (Blanchflower et al., 1991). Far from preventing reductions of the workforce, it seems that strong local unions helped to accelerate it, partly perhaps by pursuing wage increases more strongly, but more probably by making it easier for large employers to carry through and legitimate their rationalisation plans.

The Transmission of unemployment

The previous section already suggested why workers in relatively narrow, routine jobs are naturally the prime target for rationalisation. But unemployment increases in various ways, of which rationalisation of jobs is only one. Closures are particularly common during periods of recession, and they affect all kinds of employees, not just manual workers. Furthermore, there is much evidence to show that in the UK workforce reduction has largely taken the form of a reduction of recruitment. Employers contract their workforce, not so much by pushing existing employees out of their jobs, as by avoiding replacement when they leave. In this case, it is those waiting to find jobs who chiefly suffer. This partly explains why workers have continued to prefer higher wages to better chances of employment: those getting the benefit of higher wages do not, on the whole, suffer direct consequences.

These varied forms of unemployment raise further questions about the transmission of unemployment on to working-class occupations. The second main section of this chapter will describe some further mechanisms that ensure that long-term unemployment, however it occurs, remains focused on these lower occupations. The first main set of mechanisms consits in contracts and conditions of employment, while the second main set consists in the education and training systems that exist in Britain.

The conditions of manual employment

Employment contracts and conditions of employment affect the ways in which workers flow into unemployment. A great deal of recent thinking concerning problems of the labour market has focused upon the effects of these flows. The detailed ways in which people pass into and through unemployment – especially anything which affects the timing of such movements – is increasingly recognised as important. As we shall see, moving out of a job has quite different implications for manual workers by comparison with non-manual workers.

EMPLOYMENT SECURITY AND JOB TERMINATION

A simple, obvious, but generally neglected point is that manual workers, by comparison with white-collar workers, can and do lose their jobs at much shorter notice. Although, as mentioned earlier, casual employment as such has become rather unusual, most manual workers in Britain are employed on contracts or understandings of one week's notice of termination on either side. This also applies to many female workers in routine clerical or service occupations: these are often referred to, in their organisations, as weekly staff, a title which distinguishes them from those who enjoy full staff status. Conversely, higher-level administrative, technical or professional staff usually have contracts specifying at least one month's and often three months' notice of termination.

Surveys of unemployment in the 1980s revealed the extensive impact of short periods of notice during a period of economic recession (Daniel, 1990). Among skilled manual workers (the largest group entering unemployment), one quarter were given no notice whatever while 40 per cent were given notice of one week or less. Among semi-skilled manual workers, the next largest group, one third received no notice whatever while 45 per cent were given notice of one week or less. This was despite UK employment law which specifies that redundant workers must be given one week's notice for each year of service (up to a maximum of twelve). This law is widely disregarded in practice. In addition, many workers do not qualify for its protection because of short periods of employment in their jobs.

Perhaps equally important are the unwritten customs of industry, which are difficult to document statistically, but form part of shared understandings. So far as white-collar workers are concerned, many British employers tend to avoid dismissal or redundancy by unofficially suggesting to the people concerned that they should look for other jobs, and by giving them time off work to help them do this. As a result, these employees can make a move to another job in the most advantageous circumstances. This type of favourable treatment is, however, rarely extended to manual workers.

Because of these favours, as well as longer contractual notice periods, white-collar workers are generally better placed to make transitions when their jobs are coming to an end. This helps them to avoid ever appearing in unemployment. Manual workers, on the other hand, usually have too short a notice period to avoid entering unemployment, especially when vacancies are scarce so that job search has to be protracted. Once unemployed, workers may be exposed to problems of low income (making job search difficult) and to discrimination by employers, who prefer to take individuals straight from another job. Such problems increase the risks of drifting towards long-term unemployment.

EMPLOYERS' POLICIES ON SICKNESS AND RETIREMENT

The way in which employers make provision for the ill-health of workers tends to differ between manual and white-collar groups. Recently, schemes of sickness pay for manual workers have become more common in large companies, but they are still less widespread than schemes for white-collar workers. Even where sick pay schemes for manual workers exist, their provision is likely to be less extensive and less generous. Similarly, the most progressive employers provide pension schemes for all types of employee, and include provision for early retirement on grounds of ill-health or disability. But such pensions and early retirement options are, again, less often available to manual workers than to white-collar workers, at least in the UK. Further, outright dismissal for reasons of ill-health is widely practiced by employers in the case of manual workers, as can be seen from information about workers entering unemployment.

In fact, ill-health has been one of the major factors governing entry to unemployment, and more particularly long-term unemployment in Britain. A large-scale survey in the early 1980s found that one in five of long-term unemployed had lost their previous job for reasons of ill-health; and this was found to apply as much to those under 35 as to those over 35 years old. Most of the workers affected came from manual jobs. Ill-health was less common among former white-collar workers in this survey, even though on average these white-collar workers were considerably older (White, 1983).

It is important to realize that ill-health has quite a different significance once a person is unemployed. Ill-health, in most cases, consists of episodes that come to an end; the individual can recover and be capable of working effectively once again (with perhaps the need of a transfer to a different kind of job). Once out of a job, however, the problems of ill-health add to those of unemployed status: employers may be reluctant to risk recruiting a person who has recently had a serious illness. The advantage of remaining in employed status, while recovering from ill-health, is therefore a very considerable one.

EMPLOYER TRAINING AND PROMOTION POLICIES
While differences in notice periods and sickness entitlements affect manual workers' unemployment in a direct way, differences in training and promotion chances have subtler effects.

It has commonly been said that manual workers have jobs while white-collar workers have careers. British employers have generally shown little enthusiasm for training manual workers, and the apprenticeship systems (which at their best catered for only 40 per cent of young male entrants to manual work) collapsed in the late 1970s. The working-class youth culture of Britain has become one of job changing, because there has been little to be gained (in the form of training or promotion prospects) by staying in the kinds of jobs available to young, poorly qualified people. By moving from job to job, young workers could acquire experience and, at the same time, increase their short-term earnings while relieving the monotony of narrow jobs. Young entrants to white-collar occupations, on the other hand, are much more likely to receive training, have better prospects, and for the most part develop strong attachment to their employers at an early stage.

Because of frequent job changing, young people in manual occupations face severe risks of protracted unemployment when the job market becomes difficult and they are caught between jobs. Surveys have shown that about half of long-term unemployed people aged under 35 have a background of job changing and recurrent unemployment (White, 1983).

The lack of formal, recognised training in most manual jobs also weakens later chances in the job market. Once in long-term unemployment, it seems that the chances of escaping are influenced by qualifications, but not at all by training in previous jobs (unless this has led to a qualification). British employers seem to disregard training provided elsewhere, perhaps because it is not certificated and is, therefore, thought to be of doubtful quality (White and MacRae, 1989). Entry to many white-collar jobs, on the other hand, depends upon certificated training (e.g. in secretarial skills, book-keeping, travel services) as well as on educational qualifications; these certificates facilitate mobility between jobs. This point leads towards a much wider theme, which will be treated in the next section.

EMPLOYMENT CONDITIONS: OVERVIEW

Although we have discussed each aspect of manual workers' conditions of employment separately, it is not hard to see that they can be combined to form a larger pattern of employment relationships. Traditionally, employers in Britain have viewed their relations with manual workers as being, in principle, monetary and short-term. Labour is purchased in such a way as to minimise longer-term financial commitments. Accordingly, notice periods are kept short, obligations towards sickness and retirement are avoided as far as possible, and training (which implies an investment in the individual) is kept to a minimum. All this, of course, is facilitated by the design of jobs in as simple and standardised a way as possible, so that one worker's contribution can quite easily be replaced by another's. Manual workers for their part, seeing themselves as dispensable, avoid developing too much attachment to the job, and become 'mercenary' in their outlook.

This, it must be said, is an over-simplified view compared with the many nuances of reality. In the course of time, manual workers who stay with an organisation may grow in value to the employer, become trusted, and receive privileges or advantages beyond the formal employment contract. In addition, some British employers now recognise the importance of human resources at all levels of the organisation, and strive to remove distinctions in the treatment of different groups of workers, seeing them as barriers to cooperation. But these employers probably remain in a minority. In addition, the external pressures of competition may force many employers to cut costs, and may limit their ability to improve conditions of employment. Instead, their attention becomes focused upon cost reduction and the rationalisation of the labour force. The types of employment contracts and conditions applying to manual workers, as well as the nature of much of the work they do, has made them the chief candidates for this rationalisation.

Barriers to mobility: education and training policies

The process of rationalisation of manual employment has been particularly visible in the past 20 or 25 years. Economic historians (Van der Wee, 1986) have shown that in the immediate post-war period (1945–65), firms invested in new machinery chiefly to rebuild production and to meet increasing consumer demand for products. It was an age of expansion. Later, however, firms began to invest in new machinery partly to replace labour – that is, to meet a more or less static consumer demand with fewer workers. By the 1980s, the great majority of capital invested by British manufacturing firms appears to have been of this labour-saving kind (Denny and Nickell, 1991).

Not surprisingly, the proportion of manual jobs has decreased since about 1966, as has the proportion of jobs in manufacturing industry. In fact, about 5 million manual jobs disappeared over 20 years or so (see Table 1.1). But it is a mistake to assume that this, by itself, explains why unemployment for former manual workers has been rising over the period. Every country experiences continual change in the mix of different occupations and industries. For example, most countries in Europe (including Britain) have greatly reduced the proportion of people who work in agriculture, but they do not usually speak about agricultural unemployment. The former agricultural workers have, on the whole, been absorbed elsewhere in the economy. As some types of occupation decline, others emerge or increase their requirements. The all-important issue is whether workers displaced from one occupational group can successfully move into other opportunities. It is only if they cannot that unemployment results. The question to be answered, then,

Table 1.1
Change in employment in Great Britain, 1951–1987

	1951	1961	1966	1971	1981	1987
Manufacturing employment (millions)	8.7	9.0	9.2	8.6	6.1	5.1
Manual workers (millions)	14.5	14.0	14.4	13.2	11.1	9.2
Manufacturing as % of total	39	38	37	35	26	24
Manual as % of total	64	59	58	53	48	45

is why manual workers have been relatively unsuccessful in moving into new opportunities. What have been the barriers to mobility?

One such barrier is likely to be housing. A large proportion of manual workers in Britain lives in rented housing provided by the public authorities. To obtain such housing, in the British system, usually involves registering and remaining on a waiting list for several years. Rented accommodation in the private housing sector is extremely scarce. These conditions certainly make it difficult for those already in public sector housing to move from one part of the country to another in pursuit of a job. White-collar workers, on the other hand, are more frequently buying their own home, and this gives them greater freedom of movement.

But although housing is important, it clearly is not the chief barrier. Even in areas with depressed local industries, white-collar job opportunities have been growing, and yet displaced manual workers have not been able to take advantage of them. This local mismatch between the supply of skills and the supply of jobs suggests how deep are the differences between manual and non-manual jobs.

Recently, British economists have begun to analyse this kind of mismatch with the notion of entry costs (Jackman et al., 1990). In principle, workers could move from jobs where they are no longer needed to new jobs, so avoiding unemployment, but this would usually involve a cost. If the cost is too high, then the movement does not take place; people stay unemployed; the growing industry does not get the workers it needs; growth slows down; and the shortages of workers in growth areas force wages up, which may in turn increase wage inflation and adversely affect the whole economy.

The chief entry cost to a new occupation is likely to be training. Many non-manual jobs involve a fundamentally different kind of skill and qualification to most manual jobs. The costs of training would be correspondingly high. If the skills needed involve certain standards of numeracy and literacy, then employers would expect these to have been provided by the system of school education. They would not be interested in recruiting anyone who did not have basic educational qualifications. Even twenty years ago in Britain, a person with basic school qualifications was more than three times as likely to get a white-collar job as a person without those qualifications. Manual workers who have lost their jobs and have poor qualifications, facing a job market where most of the opportunities are in white-collar work, in a practical sense have nowhere to go.

Problems of education, training and qualification are, accordingly, fundamental reasons for manual unemployment. This also helps to explain why the possession of educational qualifications has been such an advantage for young people in escaping from long-term unemployment. This is, of course, a type of problem that exists in most industrial countries, but it is perhaps particularly serious in Britain because educational standards (except for the most educated 20 per cent) have been rather low. Twenty years ago, more than half the male working population (and probably a considerably greater proportion of the female population) had no qualifications whatever (Heath, 1981). Even now, nearly one half of young people enter the labour market at the age of sixteen (the minimum compulsory age of schooling). And at least one third of young people lack the kind of educational qualifications that would help them to get a white-collar job at some time in the future.

Until quite recently employers exerted little pressure upon the education system for better standards of qualification. It was accepted that the majority of school leavers would have no qualification, and they would be offered simple, routinised manual jobs with little training and few prospects. Were the poor educational standards what inhibited employers from offering training and development for manual workers? Or was it the undemanding nature of the jobs on offer, and the lack of training and development, which inhibited the raising of educational standards? British historians tend to favour the second interpretation (Barnett, 1986). At an early date, many British manufacturers turned away from the pursuit of technologically advanced products and processes, and so took little interest in the development of technical education. Manual workers did not need to be well educated or highly trained to turn out fairly simple, standardised products. The technical cadres inside companies were too limited to offer much advancement, even for skilled let alone semi-skilled workers. From this point of view, the weaknesses of the British educational system reflect long-established tendencies in British firms.

It is also clear that these tendencies still continue to exert a considerable influence on education and training. After the collapse of the British apprenticeship system, and the advent of massive youth unemployment, the Youth Training Scheme (YTS) was established to provide two years of initial work experience and training to any sixteen-year-old school leaver. The state paid an allowance to the trainees, so that employers had no wages to pay, and a direct subsidy was also paid towards training costs. Despite these benefits, it seems that many employers were still reluctant to provide training, especially training that provided general skills, which could be transferred to working elsewhere. Only about one half of the entrants to YTS stayed for two years, as they were anxious to move into a job as soon as possible. In addition, only 25–40 per cent (in various years) completed a recognised qualification through the scheme. Evidently, the opportunities for young school-leavers have remained linked chiefly to short-term jobs rather than to acquisition of skills and qualifications, which would provide upward mobility in the long run.

The explanation of manual workers' unemployment in terms of education and training can therefore be described as a series of stages, which reinforce one another. Educational attainments at school allocate young people to occupational paths, streaming those with poorer qualifications (or none) into manual work. Because the educational standards required by employers for manual jobs are low, schoolchildren expecting to enter these occupations have little incentive to do well at school. Given recruits with low educational standards, employers find training – beyond a simple level – too costly, and this limits the kind of jobs and development opportunities which young people have. When the need for cost savings arises in firms, routinised jobs, with low associated investments in training, are the ones which it is easiest to rationalise. Again, the awareness that manual jobs provide a reservoir that is relatively expendable perhaps deters management from making training investments in the first place. Finally, as manual jobs are cut, former manual workers find themselves on the job market with insufficient qualifications for the new jobs becoming available, and both employers and the state find them too costly to train for these jobs.

Conclusion

This chapter has pointed to the working-class nature of unemployment in Britain. It has also suggested that if we can explain why unemployment has been focused upon manual workers this will be a key to understanding the mass unemployment of recent years.

We have indicated a variety of factors which have contributed to working class unemployment in Britain:

- the aspirations of workers for a higher standard of living, and the wage pressures created by the policies both of their trade unions and their employers;
- the moves towards rationalisation of the labour force by employers, and the concentration of workforce reductions upon manual jobs;
- the nature of employment conditions and contracts for lower-level workers, making them vulnerable to long-term unemployment when economic conditions are unfavourable;
- workers' low levels of education and training, which restrain their personal mobility and limit the adaptability of the whole economy.

All these aspects of the problem are interconnected. For example, short notice periods and low investments in training make it more attractive for employers to focus their workforce reductions upon manual workers. A lack of long-term opportunities, coupled with a feeling of being disposable, lead manual workers to press for short-term wage increases whenever they have the chance. Again, wage pressures on the side of workers and their trade unions provoke an interest in rationalisation on the part of employers, especially when a low level of education makes alternative policies, such as a high level of innovation, difficult to pursue.

It would be possible to continue, describing further interconnections in a piecemeal way. But it may be more useful, though more difficult, to try to express in a general way the point of view which underlies the various parts of this chapter.

This viewpoint puts the emphasis upon the social dimension, although it does not ignore the facts which are of importance to economists. Like most economists, we have seen the implications of wage pressures for employment as the process most directly linked to recent unemployment. But we see bargaining over wages and employment as essentially a social matter. It is social, in the first place, because both large trade unions and large employers in Britain are too powerful to be much constrained by the competitive forces of the market-place. It is social, again, because both unions and employers take into account their own

long-term relationships – a point which has been particularly obvious in
the recent phase, when generous wage offers by leading employers have
encouraged unions to legitimate their workforce reduction policies. It is
social, furthermore, because limits to the bargaining process are set by
the local and fragmented nature of British bargaining institutions, which
have evolved over many years, reflecting the preferences of both
workers and employers, and which now make it very difficult to develop
a national level of cooperation in favour of full employment.

As part of our social view of unemployment, we also emphasise the
importance of the choices made by each type of social actor, rather than
attributing events to the impersonal action of economic forces. For
example, the picture provided in this chapter makes it clear that
manual workers, as a group, are not merely passive participants in the
events which bring about unemployment: their preferences and aspirations are an essential part of the story. To say this, however, is not to
blame the victim. For the choices of workers, like those of employers,
are shaped and circumscribed by the social divisions which have
characterised British society, including the labour market, for so long.
Individuals and groups respond to the opportunities open to them, and
in Britain these opportunities have been depressed for those from a
working-class background entering employment as manual workers
(Goldthorpe, 1980).

This chapter has described some of the differences of employment
conditions, of contractual relations, of education and of training, which
divide the lower occupations from the higher in Britain. The thought
with which we conclude is that if the divisions or differences between
manual and non-manual workers are too great, then it will be difficult
to find a stable solution to the problems of wages, jobs and unemployment, because these divisions will constitute a barrier to adaptation and
an incitement to conflict. Manual workers who have achieved a high
basic standard of education, who enjoy strong employment rights, and
who can expect long-term personal progress in their working lives,
are well placed to adapt – individually and collectively – to the new
economic order which has been emerging. It is possible to point to a
number of European countries such as Sweden where these conditions
are largely fulfilled. Britain, unfortunately, has not been one of them.
Lack of economic resilience, including mass unemployment, reflect a
failure of social adaptability, and nothing makes this so apparent as the
working-class character of British long-term unemployment.

Notes

1. The early work on unemployment by Beveridge is described in: Harris, J., 1972, *Unemployment and Politics: a study in English social policy 1886–1914*, Clarendon Press.
2. Pigou's achievement was eclipsed by Keynes but is now once again recognised as highly predictive of problems that have become significant in current conditions.
3. For a review of many of the ideas proposed, including a number of the more bizarre, see: Lindbeck and Snower, 1985.
4. See, for example, Schmidt, 1983.

CHAPTER 2

THE LONG-TERM UNEMPLOYED IN FRANCE

Odile Benoît-Guilbot with Mireille Clémençon

The rise in the unemployment rate in France since 1975 has been accompanied by an extension in the duration of unemployment, which now frequently exceeds one, two or even three years. Yet as recently as 1990 employers were complaining of a shortage of labour and difficulties in filling jobs, sometimes where only unskilled labour was called for. It would seem that often those who have been registered with Agence nationale pour l'emploi (ANPE) for more than a year are in no great hurry to apply for training courses or vacancies, particularly in building or industry. This apparent contradiction leads one to ask who bears the brunt of long-term unemployment and whether recent tendencies have changed. To what extent and under what circumstances does it happen that one category of those left in the wake of economic progress becomes socially marginalised? What role does the family play in bringing about or resisting such exclusion?

Who are the long-term unemployed?

Long-term unemployment may have been latent towards the end of the 1960s but it has only recently become a problem with the sheer scale of its development. During the prolonged phase of post-war growth and in spite of sustained full employment, there were always a certain number who had been unemployed for more than a year. In 1968, with the unemployment rate at 3 per cent, they counted for slightly fewer than 125,000 out of a total of 614,000 unemployed (i.e. 20 per cent), for the most part people in poor health and/or over 50. Twenty years later in March 1989, they numbered 878,000 (42 per cent), and those who had been unemployed for more than two years 490,000, whereas the total number of unemployed rose less sharply, nevertheless reaching 2.1 million (See Appendix for information on method). Nor was 1989 the worst year. Unemployment records were beaten between 1985 and 1987 in the case of men, and between 1986 and 1988 for women. A small improvement was recorded in 1989 and 1990, both as regards the overall volume of unemployment and its duration (cf Figure IA.1, p. 18 *et seq.*).

Breakdown by age

Unemployment and especially long-term unemployment has affected women rather than men. In 1989 their rates of unemployment of whatever duration were still higher than those for men, their rate of unemployment for a year and over being almost twice as high (5 per cent as against 2.6 per cent for men). Hence they represent 60 per cent of the unemployment figures for a year and over yet only 43 per cent of the working population. The figure has been relatively unchanged since 1982. The number of women who have been unemployed for more than a year has indeed risen in absolute terms reaching nearly 525,000, but in the same proportion as the figure for men. So their relative position has hardly altered. Figures for 1989 show only that they are slightly less prone to remaining unemployed for over two years but rather more so in the medium term, one to two years. It is true that when it becomes too difficult for them to find a job again, they are able to justify the choice of not working more readily than do men as an exit from unemployment.

Clearly the young are highly vulnerable to unemployment. Overall rates in the 15–24 age group reached unwelcome records in 1985 with 23 per cent male and 29 per cent female. By 1989 levels had fallen to 15 per cent and 22 per cent respectively (Table 2.1), which is still high and considerably higher than in most European countries (cf Table IA.4a, p. 25). The evident improvement in the situation of young people is the outcome of positive steps taken by the government to improve employment and training prospects (for first- or second-time takers).

Do young people escape long-term unemployment to a greater degree than other categories? They enter their working lives, in fact, via a succession of courses, recurrent bouts of training, casual and part-time filler jobs or fixed-term contracts, interspersed with spells of relatively short unemployment. These successive spells of employment (or pseudo-employment) and unemployment serve to mask the nevertheless real and probably under-estimated impact of long-term unemployment

Table 2.1
Unemployment rates by age, sex and grades of educational attainment
– France, 1989

Educational grade	MEN overall	≥ 1 yr	≥ 2 yrs	WOMEN overall	≥ 1 yr	≥ 2 yrs
18–29						
III	3,3	*	*	6,5	*	*
IV	8,4	*	*	13,6	*	*
V	10,1	2,1	0,9	20,5	7,1	3,0
VI + V [a]	20,3	5,9	3,2	31,4	13,3	7,3
Together	10,6	2,5	1,2	18,1	6,0	2,8
30–44						
III	1,6	*	*	3,2	*	*
IV	3,6	*	*	7,0	*	*
V	4,3	1,8	1,0	9,3	4,4	2,2
VI + V [a]	8,6	4,6	2,9	15,2	8,0	4,9
Together	5,0	2,2	1,3	9,7	4,7	2,6
45–59						
III	2,2	*	*	*	*	*
IV	2,4	*	*	*	*	*;
V	4,1	2,3	1,4	7,5	4,0	2,4
VI + V [a]	7,8	5,2	3,5	9,7	6,1	3,8
Together	5,7	3,5	2,3	8,0	4,7	2,5
18–59						
III	2,1	0,7	0,4	3,9	0,9	0,4
IV	4,8	1,1	0,5	9,6	2,9	1,2
V	6,2	1,9	1,0	13,1	5,3	2,5
VI + V [a]	10,0	5,0	3,2	15,3	8,0	4,8
Together	6,6	2,7	1,6	11,7	5,1	2,7

* Numbers insufficient to be reliable
See Appendix, p.77 *et seq.*, for grades of educational attainment

on young people (lasting as far as they are concerned one to two years rather than over two years). The rate of unemployment of over one year was invariably higher between 1982 and 1989 for the under 25s than for the over 50s, and manifestly for those between 25 and 49. The one exception concerns young men whose level dropped below that for the over 50s in 1988 and 1989. Even so these levels represent almost 3 per cent for males and over 6 per cent for females. Hence, out of the 878,000 unemployed for over a year in 1989, nearly 200,000 were under 25 and 150,000 over 50. Certainly, in France just as in Great Britain, but not as in Germany, young people find it very difficult to gain access into the labour market. The reasons for this being so are not easy to determine, for they probably have to do as much with recruitment practices and personnel management on the part of employers as with young peoples' attitudes.

With the over 50s, the rate of overall unemployment for men is very near to that for the 25–49 category (5.8 and 5.4 respectively), as against 7.3 and 10.5 in the case of women. Although the risk of entering unemployment is less for the over 50s in view of measures designed to cushion exit from the labour market – early retirement, and redundancy payments (Fonds national de l'emploi, FNE) – that of remaining unemployed for two years or more in the case of those unable to draw on these benefits is very great, very long-term unemployment rates (two years or more) representing 2.5 for men and 2.9 for women in 1989. Their rates of unemployment fell less than those of other categories during the slight upturn of 1988 to 1989 in spite of provisions adopted by the government, as if these measures were more effective in enabling the over 50s to leave than to re-enter employment (working rates among men of over 50 fell considerably during the 1980s, much more than in other European countries).

Alongside the decrease in unemployment among young people and its stabilisation in the case of older categories, the proportion of long-term unemployed in the intermediate group has increased and their position has worsened. Figures more than doubled between 1982 and 1989, moving up from 266,000 to 557,000, and now represent 60 per cent of long-term unemployment, which is almost as much as their share of the labour force (68 per cent). The proportion of long-term unemployed women in this category has always been significantly higher and remains so.

Concentration on the most educationally deprived

In France educational level attained appears to be a vital factor in determining the level and duration of unemployment. (See Appendix for classification of educational grades.) The fact of having continued studying and obtained a formal qualification affords protection against unemployment and the protraction of unemployment, even at a relatively advanced age.

Thus, with young men between 18 and 29, the overall rate of unemployment, which is only 3.3 in the top grade (baccalauréat plus two years at least), reaches 20.3 at the bottom, clearly marked out as representing the educationally deprived. While young men are more affected by short- than by long-term unemployment, the rates of unemployment of two years and more vary between 0.3 and 3.2, as selection becomes more stringent. Men in this category with very low educational achievement count for 18.2 per cent of the labour force and 50.4 per cent of the very long-term unemployed, which is an index of very high vulnerability (2.77 as against 0.26 for those at the top of the scale). See Appendix for calculation of this index.

In the case of young women of equivalent age the gap in rates of unemployment between high and low levels of educational achievement is still more alarming, overall the rates being respectively 6.5 and 31.4, and for two or more years 0.1 and 7.3. Young women who have attended university only very exceptionally remain unemployed for over a year, still more exceptionally over two years. Hence they are very few, probably not enough for their unemployment rate for two years or more to be dependable. One may question its accuracy but not its direction or relative scale.

The rejects of the educational system are vulnerable both to short- and long-term unemployment. The latter count for 17.6 per cent of the working population in this age group, yet constitute 30.5 per cent of unemployed women and 46.4 per ent of very long-term unemployed women. Hence their index of vulnerability (2.64) is slightly less high than that for young men; but the gap in the unemployment rates between the high and low school achievers provides evidence of greater inequality in regard to unemployment than is the case with men, the index of vulnerability of the high achievers being on 0.03.

With the benefit of age and work experience the schooling factor becomes less significant, but only to a very limited degree. In the age range 30–44, rates of unemployment of two years or more stretch from 0.4 to 2.9 for men and from 0.5 to 4.9 for women in terms of educational attainment. Indices of vulnerability for the lowest achievers are 2.16 in the case of men and 1.87 in that of women. Beyond 45 the persistent unemployment of the lowest school achievers decreases more for men than for women, both overall and very long-term; but it still remains significantly high, indices of vulnerability for unemployment lasting two years or more being 1.51 for men and 1.33 for women.

This analysis shows the importance of educational attainment throughout working life. The greater the length of unemployment, the more it falls on those whose schooling has left them without anything to show for it. Or, put another way, the lower the achievement at school, the less the chance of re-entering (or entering) employment, particularly for women.

These figures cannot fail to raise questions about the effectiveness of the French educational system, the subordination of the labour market to school selection processes, and the consequences notably on long-term unemployment. An alleviation of this concentration in the case of those over thirty might encourage the hope that young people whose training has been neglected can acquire some skill or ability when their school careers have been unsuccessful. But another less optimistic interpretation seems more plausible when one knows that employers' requirements and the demands of the job set criteria whereby recruitment becomes increasingly selective. Instead of resolving itself, as might have been the case in the past, the situation is likely to persist as young people get older, because unemployment among young people who were low achievers at school coexists with a shortage of manpower, one that cannot be made good by taking-on or training the young who are marginalised by the school system. Nor is the problem itself a peripheral one. Roughly 18 per cent of young people between 18 and 30 of employable age leave school without qualifications, this percentage has gone unchanged for several years.[1]

Worsening situation for the less qualified

As does educational attainment, occupational categories[2] lead to very marked variations in unemployment rates (Table 2.2). The unskilled (manual workers or those in trade or in low-grade personal service jobs) are the worst hit, senior management and middle-grade occupations the least. The self-employed – in trade, craft industries or farming – can be classified somewhat awkwardly with wage-earners, whose unemployment rates are spaced out at intervals on a line between unskilled workers and management. Self-employed men or women have one of the lowest entry rates into unemployment, but are highly subject to long-standing unemployment. For the purposes of this analysis we include only wage-earners and those in the professions.

Between 1982 and 1986–7 all categories in different degrees sustained a rise in unemployment, but they did not all benefit to the same degree from the improved situation in 1988–9. Those at managerial level displayed resilience, finding themselves in 1989 with unemployment rates that were substantially the same as they had experienced in 1982, however long the spell (figures for men: overall unemployment 2.7, long-term 0.9; women: overall 4.0, long-term 1.3). Hence they benefited very largely from the recovery in growth, so much so that there was talk of a dearth of labour in this sector.

On the other hand, the concentration of long-term and very long-term unemployment on unskilled workers and employees became extremely pronounced among men and women alike. For example, their unemployment rate for a year or more rose from 3.1 to 5.0 (men) and from 5.2 to 8.9 (women); for two years or more, from 1.2 to 3.1 (men) and from 2.3 to 5.0 (women). The gap between them and management widened considerably: in the case of two and more years unemployment, the 1989 rate in regard to the unskilled is eight times higher than that for management; in 1982 it was only three times higher.

The index of vulnerability throws further light on the concentration of unemployment on the unskilled. In the 18 to 59 age group, unskilled men number only 17 per cent of the working population but 37 per cent of the very long-term unemployed (index of vulnerability: 2.18); unskilled women, 28 per cent of the working population but 55 per cent of the very long-term unemployed (index of vulnerability: 1.96).

Other categories occupy intermediate positions between management and unskilled labour; their unemployment rates all rose by about half, but unemployment over two years more than doubled. There are two exceptions to this: female employees in administration for whom very long-term unemployment figures rose less than elsewhere, and male skilled workers, among whom unemployment of over two years rose very considerably though less so than for unskilled. The difficulty found by skilled workers in re-entering employment is corroborated by numerous reports of individual cases. Skilled workers cling to the professional identity they have established in the course of their careers and have trouble discarding it. Iribarne's view (1990b) of the importance accorded in France to the 'logic of status', precluding a self-demeaning stance, seems to be confirmed by the evidence of continuing unemployment among skilled workers.

To try to find an explanation for such high rates among those who are least qualified and most educationally deprived, one has to look either at labour supply or at the demand for labour. In regard to supply, economic and technological changes require a more organic form of cooperation within and between work teams, hence constantly increasing skills. Employers are therefore prompted only to recruit people who are able to take on responsibility, analyse problems encountered in the course of the job and communicate their experience to others. Whether for reasons that are real or imaginary, in their opinion the educationally deprived do not meet these conditions; they are no longer reckoned capable of adapting to the permanent and increasingly rapid changes in production methods. What is therefore demanded by way of social competence leads employers to cut costs by relying on criteria of educational selection in order to recruit and train new entrants and acclimatise them to the discipline (or culture) of the firm. Indeed in industry more than in the services sector the level of training and competence in the work force has clearly increased as well as wage levels. Has it become a case of taking on workers who

Table 2.2
1982–1989: Unemployment rates by occupational category

	Management and intermediate occupations	Administrative personnel	Skilled manual workers	Unskilled manual and non-manual workers
MEN				
1982				
Overall unemployment rate	2,7	3,0	5,7	10,1
Unemployment rate > 1 year	0,9	1,0	1,6	3,1
Unemployment rate > 2 years	0,4	0,5	0,6	1,2
1989				
Overall unemployment rate	2,7	4,7	8,6	13,0
Unemployment rate > 1 year	0,9	1,8	3,9	5,0
Unemployment rate > 2 years	0,4	1,1	2,3	3,1
WOMEN				
1982				
Overall unemployment rate	3,9	6,6	12,0	13,5
Unemployment rate > 1 year	1,4	2,2	5,2	5,2
Unemployment rate > 2 years	0,6	0,9	1,9	2,3
1989				
Overall unemployment rate	4,0	9,2	15,1	19,7
Unemployment rate > 1 year	1,3	3,4	7,7	8,9
Unemployment rate > 2 years	0,6	1,5	4,2	5,0

Source: Drawn from INSEE (Central Statistical Office) data and surveys on employment field: working population of all ages, including national service conscripts

are overqualified in relation to the real demands of the task? No study has apparently been made of the problem.

As regards the demand for labour, failure at school is due largely to the social legacy of the past – a younger generation growing up in a deprived milieu, where education and the acquisition of skills have no place, and in areas and localities that are more or less marginalised. This points to a flaw in the socialisation of young people for which all authorities bear responsibility – family, school, neighbourhood and television. The social norms, the value attributed to work and effort, and the instrumental link between work and consumption, which provide the basis of productivist society, have not been internalised nor have the skills needed been acquired at the opportune moment. Parted from social norms, there is no salvation at school nor in employment.

Thus long-term unemployment clearly shows that there is no way round the social stratification of French society, reinforced as it is by the educational system and competition for employment. Still more than overall employment, long-term unemployment resembles a cardgame in which all the social agents with strategic resources at their disposal force those with a weaker hand to bear the economic or technological cost of restructuring or transformation. Each one discards unemployment on to whoever near him is worse off.

Does this suggest the emergence of an underclass, an impoverished and virtually illiterate social stratum, marginalised by its impoverishment and failure to achieve under the school system or at work? This hypothesis has been advanced by writers in Britain. Before replying to the question, two remarks are called for. First, it needs to be recognised that in the post-war 'golden age' against a background of full employment and an abundant supply of jobs demanding slight or no skills, there were always pockets of poverty that resisted all attempts to eliminate them on the part of those committed to social justice. There is no doubt at all that this stratum has expanded given the current shortage of unskilled labour. Yet the phenomenon itself is no newer than the fact of poverty, it is merely the development of a condition that has always existed among those who lack the most rudimentary school and vocational qualifications. At the same time the very fact that the number of people so affected is on the increase has made the social problem more acute. The implementation of a minimum welfare payment, revenue minimum d'insertion (RMI) has no purpose other than to provide some means of survival and perhaps of finding work or a measure of social integration for these economic outcasts. Second, this deprived category represents only 45 per cent of those unemployed for over a year. The remaining 55 per cent are spread among categories that have benefited more from their schooling and possess some vocational qualifications (i.e. about 471,000 in the 18–59 age range, 167,500 of them skilled manual workers). Do they too risk being dragged down sooner or later by this new underclass predicted by social observers in Britain? If they are without support from their families, their income is likely to fall below the poverty line. It is with these people in mind that one can talk of 'new poverty', in the sense of economic poverty associated with a degree of educational or vocational attainment; and if they have children, what will they transmit to them?

The family provides shelter from unemployment or else accumulates and transmits deprivation

The family can be the best thing in the world or it can be the worst. This commonly recognised truth is borne out in the matter of unemployment. The family can consolidate its strength and the intelligence at its disposal and find a job for husbands or for wives or grown-up children when they are unemployed. It can provide its members with the confidence required for finding employment. Conversely, it can accumulate its members' disadvantages and pass them on to the following generation – low educational and vocational achievement, social isolation, inadequate initiation in making the most of one's assets, residing in a locality where the effects of the recession are particularly marked. What factors determine whether the family is a force for protection or merely multiplies handicaps?

Men married or living with a partner: less unemployment and less long-term unemployment

Male partners, married or not, escape unemployment – and long-term unemployment – more than the rest, even if the upsurge in unemployment between 1982 and 1989 affected them rather more than previously: 3.4 per cent in 1982, 4.3 per cent in 1989.[3] Table 2.3 is clear: whether one takes the rate of overall unemployment for one year and over or for more than two years, it is invariably lower for married men. According to the indices of vulnerability to long-term unemployment, they almost always emerge unscathed, though in differing degrees determined by age, job category or partner's occupation. For instance, between 30 and 44, the age of maturity and family responsibilities, their exposure is at its lowest (0.51). They do enter unemployment, but less

Table 2.3
Position within family
unemployment and vulnerability rate*

	All categories			Unskilled manual and non-manual workers (individual categories)		
	Overall rate	Unemployment rate ≥ 2 yrs	Index of vulnerability unempl. ≥ 2 yrs	Overall rate	Unemployment rate ≥ 2 yrs	Index of vulnerability unempl. ≥ 2yrs
Male partner	4,3	1,0	0,66	10,0	3,0	0,90
Female partner	10,4	2,6	0,95	19,4	5,3	0,99
Grown-up child (M), 18–29 yrs	16,5	3,3	2,09	19,1	3,0	0,89
Grown-up child (F), 18–29 yrs	21,6	3,8	1,37	24,0	4,9	0,91
Single male	8,9	2,6	1,64	14,7	5,3	1,59
Single female	7,7	1,7	0,64	17,1	4,5	0,84
Lone mother	16,2	4,4	1,61	28,0	8,2	1,52

* Index of vulnerability is, to each category, the ratio of % of its long-term unemployed to its % in the labour force.

Source: Compiled by Odile Benoît-Guilbot from INSEE (1989) survey on employment

frequently and they escape from it more swiftly (unemployment rate: 3.6 per cent; for over two years: 0.7 per cent).

Nevertheless, in the case of unskilled workers and employees (Table 2.3) vulnerability to unemployment rises (index: 0.90) and even married men experience the same difficulties in finding a first job or a new job as others in this category do, but in their case less so.

The relatively privileged situation of the man who is married or who lives with a partner, with responsibility for a family which takes up a large part if not all of his earnings, corresponds to the traditional family model. Have these family men so internalised the norms of productivist society that, unlike those who have not founded a family, they are likely to search for new employment with far more single-mindedness (or be prepared to accept less favourable conditions, the economists would say, but this is uncertain) and find it fairly rapidly, however long welfare payment lasts? Or else – and there is no contradiction here – does their acceptance of prevailing social norms act as a signal to employers who expect greater cooperation from them and a more responsible attitude to their work?

With couples the unemployment of one adds to the unemployment of the other

The built-in 'protection' of the man depends to a great degree on his partner's situation in the labour market. When she has a job, the man is still better protected; he is less often unemployed and less often does unemployment last more than two years (Table 2.4). However, when his partner is unemployed, this protection no longer operates; quite the reverse, the male partner's vulnerability is disproportionately heightened, his two rates of unemployment more than double. When his partner forgoes employment to stay at home, there is median vulnerability.

The same pattern can be observed, at higher levels of unemployment, with the unskilled (Table 2.4). In this case, the long-term rate of unemployment is more than three times as high when the female partner is unemployed.

The opposite effect is equally true and even more pronounced if one considers the male partner's working pattern. The rates in the case of women here are median (Table 2.5): 10.4 for overall unemployment and 2.6 for unemployment over two years (only single women have rates that are less high). When the male partner is working, their unemployment rates are slightly less high (9.5 and 2.2). But when he is

Table 2.4
Male (18–59 yrs) unemployment rate in
terms of partner's situation

	All categories		Unskilled manual and non-manual	
	overall	≥ 2 yrs	overall	≥ 2 yrs
Partner employed	3,0	0,6	6,8	1,6
Partner unemployed	11,1	2,6	18,8	5,4
Partner non-working	5,2	1,5	11,3	4,1
Male partners jointly	4,3	1,0	10,0	3,0

Source: Compiled by Odile Benoît-Guilbot from INSEE (1989) suvey on employment

unemployed, these rates rise dramatically to 30.2 and 8.5. This remains the case whatever the job category. The same trend and the same increase in scale are found with skilled non-manual workers (see Table 2.5).

Thus, unemployment has a distressing tendency to become compounded where couples are concerned. The likelihood of both partners finding themselves unemployed together and for a long term is considerably higher than the combination of overall probabilities of each one taken separately being in this situation. This pattern occurs with unskilled as well as with skilled non-manual workers, who are not however in high-risk categories. Even so, this cumulative effect has to be seen in perspective. The number of couples where both partners are unemployed together is very small: roughly 75,000 couples all job categories combined, and between 25,000 and 45,000 among unskilled

Table 2.5
Female (18–59) unemployment rate
in terms of partner's activity

	All categories		Unskilled manual and non-manual	
	overall	≥ 2 yrs	overall	≥ 2 yrs
Partner employed	9,5	2,2	18,0	4,4
Partner unemployed	30,2	8,5	38,9	12,4
Partner non-working			19,9	9,8
Female partners jointly	10,4	2,6	19,4	5,3

Source: Compiled by Odile Benoît-Guilbot from INSEE (1989) survey on employment

workers, according to whether one takes the man's or the woman's occupation; about 14,000 in the case of skilled non-manual workers.

This cumulative effect of both employment and unemployment where two people live together demands some explanation. First, it needs to be said that it is relatively less frequent in France than in other European countries. Further, one might have expected the opposite effect to occur. A combined strategy on the part of couples might have brought about a distribution of employment and unemployment between one partner and the other so as to reduce the impact of unemployment on the family (insofar as it is clearly not beyond the bounds of possibility to find a job corresponding with the skills of one or other of the two concerned). Indeed, there would appear to be no compensation strategy on the part of non-working wives.[4] Perhaps what is true for them is equally true for unemployed husbands.

'*Qui se ressemble s'assemble*': This tendency for like to go with like in marriage still more than in cohabitation is well established – the partners being linked by their social background, their schooling and vocational aptitudes. If there are differences between one and the other they are generally negligible, the woman's accomplishments being at a slightly lower level than the man's. Is the similarity within their relationship capable of providing an explanation for this cumulative effect?

For example, such couples may live in areas that are more economically depressed than others and where the rates of unemployment are higher than the national average. The same might hold for those who are highly skilled; but the data used here will not allow the hypothesis to be tested.

An attempt has also been made to explain the cumulative effect of unemployment in terms of the blocking of access to information that would be of assistance in finding a job. It is assumed that the partner and he/she alone through his/her job is the channel for such information, which hardly seems realistic. The nexus of the family continues to exist however strained by prolonged unemployment. Hence lack of access would suggest that families are already isolated and socially excluded.

Further to these explanations, it is entirely plausible that there is room for an interpretation that relies on attitude of mind or patterns of behaviour. The case of skilled non-manual workers can only confirm this. Partners in certain cases appear to share characteristics that statistics fail to reveal, and which cause them to be rejected by employers and/or pursue their search for a job without much conviction. It is not uncommon for a family pattern to emerge in the course of shared experience and the difficulties of everyday living, one which fails to accord with the dominant work ethic. A pattern of this sort might consist of fairly negative attitudes towards work together with a lack of consumption goals, whereas the fact of obtaining a job presupposes a positive drive in which the resolve to satisfy such goals has a part (Benoît-Guilbot, 1990). It may also be a means of rationalising the impossibility of finding work. Sooner than speak of a 'non-productivist' model, one should speak of a failure to assimilate the prevailing 'productivist' model. Low social integration of this kind is the fruit or else the cause of becoming progressively marginalised by a society that 'produces results'. An ideology that calls the industrial establishment into question might even provide an alternative model, particularly among qualified non-manual employees. But these hypotheses await verification and they barely affect the mass of long-term unemployed.

The reproduction of the family pattern in 'grown-up children'

'Grown-up children' between 18 and 29 of either sex who live with their parents, unlike the same age group with different family circumstances, display marked vulnerability to unemployment of two years or more (Table 2.3). This is evident both in the rates of unemployment in terms of duration and in the index of vulnerability to very long-term unemployment: 1.59 for male grown-up children, 1.34 for female, as against 0.36 for male partners in the same age group and 0.96 for female partners (only single mothers have greater vulnerability). This particularity of grown-up children is generally given a simple explanation, though one not easily amenable to proof, namely that their inability to find a job leads them to remain with their parents as long as they are unemployed. However this explanation could work the other way: they are unemployed simply because they can live with their parents; there is no pressing need for them to look for a job. In fact, the truth seems rather more complex.

In the first place, young people in this age group who are at work do not necessarily move away from the family home. According to the occupational status of the head of the household, between 28 per cent and 48 per cent of grown-up children stay with their families even though they have a job.

When both parents are at work, one might also expect the children to make the most of agreeable living conditions and delay entry into employment and so prolong the passage into adult life. In fact this is not at all what happens. Young people in these circumstances are more often than others still studying; they are less often jobless but mainly they are less often unemployed and less vulnerable to long-term unemployment. When their mothers are out of work, or do not work[5] but the father does, entry into employment falls off; rates of employment and inactivity increase and pursuit of studies declines. When neither parent is in employment, these tendencies become more marked. On the other hand, it is quite remarkable that when the mother has a job and the father is unemployed or non-working, the vulnerability of young people to unemployment and inactivity tends to be almost as low as when both parents are working.[6] Manifestly it is the fact of the mother's being at work that determines the childrens' low vulnerability and assists them in finding a job, whether they are boys or girls (Table 2.6).

The occupational status of the head of the family does not affect the tendency for the pattern to reproduce and multiply. It is apparent among unskilled and skilled non-manual alike, as in single-parent families – this being the mother in the vast majority of cases – and even if the unemployment rates of the children are appreciably different (Tables 2.7 and 2.8).

Overall and long-term unemployment are indeed then a family affair, whether one is talking of couples or grown-up children. But homogamy and the social legacy of social disadvantages are not in themselves

Table 2.6
Grown-up children (18–29 yrs): unemployment rate
in terms of degree of activity of parents

	Overall unemploy-ment	Unemploy-ment ≥ 1 yr	Index of vulnerability to unemployment ≥ 1 yr
Two parents			
– Both working	13,3	3,2	0,58
– Father working, mother unemployed or non-working	19,0	5,3	0,96
– Father unemployed or non-working, mother working	(15,5)*	(2,7)*	(0,48)*
– Both unemployed or non-working (18–59)	26,5	8,9	11,62
Lone parent			
– working	19,0	(4,2)*	(0,77)*
– unempl. or non-wkg.	28,8	11,1	2,01
Taken together	19,2	5,6	-

* Figure too low for % to be entirely reliable.

Source: Compiled by Odile Benoît-Guilbot from INSEE (1989) survey on unemployment

Table 2.7
Unemployment rate of grown-up children
(< 30 yrs male and female)

	Head of household unskilled			Head of household skilled		
	Overall	Unemployment rate ≥ 1 yr	Index of vulnerability unemployment ≥ 1 yr	Overall unemployment rate	Unemployment rate ≥ 1 yr	Index of vulnerability unemployment ≥ 1 yr
Two parents						
– Both working	17,7	5,4	0,85	11,9	2,4	0,68
– Father working, mother unemployed or non-working	26,1	6,3	1,0	15,5	4,1	1,13
– Father unemployed or non-working, mother working	(2,9)	(0)	–	(1,9)	–	(0)
– Both unemployed or non-working (18–59)	(43,7)	(13,2)	(2,11)	(23,9)	–	(0)
Lone parent						
– working	21,6	(3,2)	(0,50)	20,6	5,2	1,46
– Unemployed or non-working	(39,4)	13,6	(2,15)	(42,9)	(6,2)	(1,64)
Taken together	25,0	6,3	–	15,3	3,6	–

Table 2.8
Rates of unemployment, inactivity and continuing study of grown-up children (< 30 yrs male and female)

	Head of household unskilled			Head of household skilled		
	Employment rate	Inactivity rate	Educational attainment rate	Employment rate	Inactivity rate	Educational attainment rate
Two parents						
– Both working	43,2	(1,5)	40,2	25,0	(1,1)	66,9
– Father working, mother unemployed or non-working	41,2	(4,0)	35,5	29,6	(1,8)	58,5
– Father unemployed or non-working, mother working	(47,2)	(5,9)	(45,4)	(40,0)	–	(57,5)
– Both unemployed or non-working (18–59)	(31,5)	(7,5)	(30,9)	(26,7)	(4,7)	(60,2)
Lone parent						
– working	44,3	(5,6)	34,6	33,0	2,8	51,5
– Unemployed or non-working	(38,4)	(8,9)	(24,1)	(20,5)	(2,0)	(52,1)
Taken together	41,6	4,3	35,6	28,6	1,6	61,1

sufficient to account for the multiplier effect, either among the unskilled or even less among the skilled, where whatever their age the handicaps are minimal. Reference has been made to the reduced effectiveness of information sources when one member of a family is unemployed, but then why should the sources available to the mother have special significance? And why only occupational sources? Does it need one member of the family to suffer long-term unemployment for the other sources available to all its members to become ineffective? This would be tantamount to admitting that the long-term unemployment of one member necessarily entails the social isolation of the entire family and that such isolation or settlement for a mismatching work environment can account for long-term unemployment. Such an explanation requires evidence to sustain it.

Less constricting than an interpretation in terms of channels of communication and the information they transmit is the notion of a family pattern relating to work, employment and consumption, which has been mentioned in relation to partners, reproducing itself from one generation to the next. That such a notion can in part explain the problems of entering the labour market and long-term unemployment encountered by different members becomes entirely plausible. All the arguments put forward in regard to couples are relevant here and find confirmation in transmission to the children.

The all-important role of the mother's employment provides a further element. For the fact of the father having a job conforms to the norm, it does not imply deliberate choice, and the male partner to a large extent escapes unemployment. On the other hand, in spite of the manifest tendency for more and more married women to be at work, the act of choosing to take a job or, if unemployed, trying to find another one involves on the part of a mother a deliberate decision, especially so if she has young children to care for.[7] For the mother to be in a job (and not without one) is doubtless the sign that the family (including the male partner) has assimilated the norms of a society geared to production and consumption and that she is passing them on to the children.

Low levels of aptitude throughout the family, long-term unemployment, no other individual in stable employment, lack of a model setting a value on work as a vehicle at least, self-transmission from one generation to the next and persistent economic and cultural poverty, these all constitute the essential characteristics of an underclass. But in France, even if there are signs of a combination of all these features occurring in some families, they are very few, too few[8] to allow one to talk of the existence of a new social stratum. There are many poor households, designated as such because they call upon welfare services. But unemployment is probably not the essential key to the condition of poverty. It fails to account for a large majority of cases of poverty (Déchaux, 1990); in these, so far as the under 50s are concerned, long-term unemployment is symptomatic rather of preexisting problems, such as ill-health, instability or drink, which have always been linked with the descent into poverty. The scarcity of jobs and the difficulties the unskilled have in getting regular work do not beget a new class of poverty, rather, on the basis of stock situations, they increase the number of households affected. It needs to be borne in mind that most of the poor are out of employment not unemployed.

Nevertheless, if the cumulative family factor is insufficient to establish such an underclass, permanently excluded from employment and an acceptable standard of living, at an individual level, there is a not inconsiderable chance that the long-term unemployed may initially face joblessness for a time at least, especially when they are both low school achievers and without vocational qualifications. They may relinquish the symbolic link they have with society – their registration at the job centre. For as long as they are unemployed their benefits are poor because of their previous wage and in many cases the precarious nature of former jobs. The possibility of moving from non-activity into poverty are very high among unemployed who live alone, as is the case with 16 per cent of those who have been unemployed for over a year (including single mothers). The rest live in households consisting of several people. The various allowances and support from the family, in particular support from those, if they exist, who work and have a job, are in most cases a means of counteracting the slide into poverty.

Assessment of the drop in expenditure in working people's households when one member is unemployed is manifestly imprecise, varying between 15 per cent and 27 per cent depending on how it is calculated, types of household (Herpin, 1992). With the lower figure, difficulties are real enough but can be overcome; with the higher, contraction of the budget by a quarter in households already deprived begins to pose serious problems. Moreover, expenses are less readily contractable than resources, so that when unemployment persists the economic situation of families can become precarious. In fact, the estimation of variations in family income according to the number and position of unemployed in the family and the length of unemployment is complex and apparently has not yet been undertaken. The connection between poverty and unemployment is very little known.

There remains the problem of qualified non-manual employees who in theory have attained an educational level that allows them to escape long-term unemployment. The absence of cultural deprivation in this instance presents a problem; it clearly prevents them from being assimilated into an underclass. It is true that some of them receive income support. It is difficult to see how those who are qualified, the young in particular, can put up with a condition of unemployment and persistent poverty. In their case the passage into adult life is likely to be prolonged and involve resourcefulness in relying on transfer incomes such as unemployment benefit or income support (RMI) more or less prompted by an alternative model of relating to the labour market and the consumer society. In respect of this group, and this group only, one could speak of 'new poverty', a form of poverty which might possibly not be lasting.

Conclusion

After a year's unemployment, those who remain unemployed and whom we have called long-term unemployed no longer resemble, in their social standing and proficiency, those – some 87 per cent – who having entered unemployment exited rapidly. The criteria set by employers in regard to job vacancies are ruthlessly selective in their application, passing over any whose qualifications, vulnerability or frailness fail to satisfy them or who have given up when they repeatedly get nowhere in their efforts at job searching. Differentiation between the unemployed has no doubt always existed, but it has become more marked during the last ten years. Following a brief period of transformation, during which unemployment, including long-term unemployment, reached more or less everyone, French society targeted deprived categories for persistent unemployment. These categories are caught in a trap and have not benefited from the recovery in growth. A long stretch of unemployment becomes a stigma that stands in the way of a return to work.

Low school achievement and lack of vocational qualifications commonly characterise the majority of long-term unemployed, though these can be compounded by age, sex, family circumstances and so on. It would seem that the generation of the baby boom, producing higher school achievers than their elders, closed ranks over these ten years so as to keep their jobs and shift the burden of unemployment on to their weaker brethren. The median rise in levels of education has created a divide between low achievers at school and those who followed a normal course of studies, bearing in mind that not all qualifications rapidly open the door to a job. Failure to achieve at school and eventual exclusion from the labour market are often discernible in the first years of primary school. The question arises as to why nothing is done until young people are sixteen and the failure to provide them with a practical form of training is complete. If some of the measures to relieve long-term unemployment have been adopted with an eye to political or media advantage, hence dictated by short-term considerations, others can command a longer perspective and tackle the root of the problem. It is to be hoped that higher educational standards will come to benefit everyone and that the baccalauréat will be accessible to 80 per cent of every generation, but only so long as this does not block the social and employment possibilities of the remaining 20 per cent who will not and cannot make the grade. In the light of observations made in this chapter, the need to come to grips early with the problem of non-achievement at school seems fundamental so as to reduce long-term unemployment and the prospects of marginalisation it contains.

As for the unskilled – who are often also the less educated – they are the victims of transformations in the system of production which has its own logic. To a greater extent than elsewhere French society, embracing as it did time-and-motion study methods in industry, produced workers whose jobs were fragmented and deprived of initiative and who acquiesced to the extent that their intellectual attainment was low. In Germany the division of labour was less extreme, work tasks more complex and autonomous. There are societal reverberations here in line with what Maurice *et al.* (1979) have described in their comparison between France and Germany. The contrast between the two countries is also apparent in a breakdown of those in long-term unemployment, with few unskilled in Germany and many in France.

Therefore, production methods have changed. New jobs in industry are no longer fragmented and machine-like, rather they assume a level of competence beyond the reach of the unskilled. In the services sector too, unskilled work has not developed as much as it has elsewhere. In the view of Iribarne (1990a) the 'logic of honour', the feeling for status that characterises interpersonal relationships in France, accounts for this relative resistance to change. Jobs in the tertiary sector appear to be thought of as servile' or degrading and, wherever possible, are replaced by machines or self-service. Hence there is a severe shortage of unskilled employment, which is nevertheless needed by the unemployed who lack training, for the reason that adult training schemes, which have been so difficult to set up in industry, are doubtless not a panacea in the eyes of public opinion and the decision-makers.

We have pointed to the degree of diversity among the long-term unemployed, both as individuals, which determines their strength or lack of strength on the labour market, and in regard to their family situation and the economic status of others in the family unit (see Appendix Table 2A.1). Frequently there is no point of comparison in their circumstances. What is there in common between a self-taught forty-five year old manager, a married woman with young children whose husband has a secure job, a youth with no educational qualifications born of parents on the dole or an average young couple with no children, beyond their having been at least a year without employment and failing – or not always trying very hard – to find it? Yet if they do not all receive benefit, they are virtually all registered with ANPE and this requires a positive, repeated gesture. Maintaining this link, although a symbolic one, with the world of labour proves that the split with productive society has not occurred and that marginalisation is not complete. That is to be found elsewhere, among some of those who don't even claim – or claim no longer – to be looking for work, or who no longer reregister, if they have ever registered, with ANPE, like most of those entitled to income support. This albeit symbolic link, which grants minimal status to the unemployed, to some of them at least (Schnapper, 1989), should give pause for reflection to those whose mission it is to root out the bogus unemployed. Indeed what merit has political obsession with the rate of unemployment in comparison with the risk of exclusion not merely from work but from the ranks of job-seekers, in other words with the risk of still greater marginalisation for those who cannot find work on account of their age, lack of qualification, physical and mental health or geographical locality simply because there are not enough jobs for which they are fitted?

Along with the deprived there is a further category of those who fail to exit from unemployment in spite of being less destitute in terms of schooling and skills. Either they have an alternative social model in relating to work, or they have personal problems which the ordeal of job-searching brings into the open. More particularly in the first case, one can comprehend their readiness to go along with what is required of them by the employment apparatus and in the matter of benefit (so long as they are under 50), because in 1989 these unemployed tended to find themselves encountering a labour shortage. Economists have been unable to give conclusive demonstration of the role played by welfare benefit in preventing the return to work; the evidence points to its being instrumental only in the case of those whose wages were high before being unemployed, hence of the least disadvantaged. All things considered, if long-term unemployment does not generate protest and demonstrations, it must be because a majority of long-term unemployed (75 per cent according to Table 2A.1) are with families whose support may well enable them to withstand the economic, psychological and social effects of their being unemployed – with the exception, that is, of those families with whom unemployment and disadvantages multiply and are passed on.

Notes

1. In working on the 1989 survey on employment we have studied only those in the 18–59 age range, hence our figures may differ slightly from those of INSEE.
2. Even in INSEE's survey on employment, the numbers of unemployed are not invariably sufficient for close analysis of their characteristics. We have therefore grouped together categories where there were similarities both in regard to level and length of unemployment and to educational attainment.
3. For 1982, cf Coeffic, N., p. 82. For 1989, INSEE survey on employment (1989) in the study made by Odile Benoît-Guilbot.
4. As observed by N. Herpin (1990) in following a cohort of unemployed over a period of two years, the female partner giving no hint at all of intending to take a new or another job, even if only to register with ANPE as looking for work.
5. These two categories have been grouped together since their effect on the childrens' situation is very similar.
6. A tendency that recurs in the same way with different gender and occupational categories. But the number of couples is insufficient for the tendency to be authenticated, in particular when analysing sub-groups.
7. For a female partner with young children, one means of resolving the tension between family and occupational obligations is to remain in unemployment for a time.
8. Given that, for the purposes of the present study, only the 18–59 age range has been taken, it is reasonable that the assessment of households in difficulty should be lower than that made in 1986 by CREDOC (Centre de recherches d'études et de documentation sur la consommation).

Appendix

Three observations as to method

1. The labour market applies different rules and regulations in the case of men and in the case of women. This divergence requires data involving gender to be treated separately wherever possible. In dealing with unemployment, in particular, gender grouping would simply bring obscurity and confusion into the discussion.

2. In order to establish numbers of unemployed and time spent in unemployment two sources are available: particulars of job seekers who have signed on with ANPE and the annual INSEE labour force survey. In neither instance do the numbers quite correspond, nor are the figures used precisely the same. It would take too long to go into why this is so, but the differences are not to be seen as errors. We have preferred to adopt the INSEE source, first because it takes the actual situation of the unemployed person into account, thereby following the norms laid down by the ILO, however questionable these may appear (ANPE in fact sets out the administrative position of the person concerned, yet, as it happens, the regulations here are such that long-term unemployment is clearly underestimated compared with INSEE.) Second, the INSEE surveys of employment are far more rewarding as sources of information on individuals and their families and provide more scope for analysis. We have resorted in particular to the 1989 survey with the purpose of making a systematic study of those within the 18–59 age range. Computerised data from the survey were kindly made available to us by the Laboratoire d'analyse secondaire et de méthodes appliquées en sociologie (LASMAS) of the IRESCO research and development section of the CNRS (IRESCO, Institut de recherche sur les sociétés contemporaines). Our study was limited to those between ages 18 and 59 and this accounts for some divergence between our figures and those published by INSEE. Information from 1990 and 1991 was not available when this chapter was being written.

3. The starting point for most of the longitudinal sets happens to be 1982, although the span is relatively short. But it is only then that the terminology and methods of reckoning become uniform. The cut-off point in most cases is 1989, detailed figures for 1990 and 1991 not being available at the time of writing.

Educational grades

In France the abundance of degrees, diplomas and certificates of a vocational or more general nature, and their wide variation in terms of years makes it difficult to apply a scale that is not age-related. We opted for the higher administrative scale, which is divided into seven grades, even though, in a country wedded to formal qualifications, it is based on the grade attained rather than the formal attribution. We chose to classify the scale into four groups:

1. Grades I and II: numbers of students obtaining a first or further degree from a university or *grande école*; Grade III: numbers of students obtaining a two year (post-baccalauréat) diploma from an IUT, a higher vocational training certificate (brevet de technicien supérieur BTS), nursing or other other medical diploma, primary school teacher-training diploma, or who have completed the first two years of degree studies (Diplômes d'études universitaires générales, DEUG).

2. Grade IV: numbers of students who have completed the final baccalauréat

year in the upper school and those who have abandoned post-baccalauréat studies before reaching Grade III.

3. Grade V: numbers of students who have completed the final year of a technical or vocational course or an apprenticeship scheme as well as those who abandoned upper school studies before the final stage.

4. Grade VI: those who have completed a middle school non-academic syllabus leading to an apprenticeship or allied scheme or a one-year vocational course; Grade Va: those who leave at the level of *3e* or who leave technical/vocational classes before the final year and those who withdraw during apprenticeship.

Calculation of index of vulnerability for long- or very long-term unemployment

For any category taken this index represents the ratio of its percentage among long-term unemployed (or very long-term as the case may be) to its percentage in the labour force. A one for one unit equivalence indicates that the place of long-term unemployed is strictly proportional to that of the particular category in the labour force. One for > 1 indicates that the proportion of long-term unemployed is higher than its proportion in the labour force (i.e. unemployment in this category is excessive) Conversely, one for < 1 indicates that the proportion of unemployment is lower than its labour force proportion (i.e. the category is sheltered from unemployment).

Table 2A.1

Long-term unemployed (> 1yr) aged between 18 and 59 as
percentage of number of long-term unemployed 1989

1 – sex		**5 – position in**	
Men	40	**family**	
women	60	Male partners	20
		Female partners	39
2 – age		Grown-up children	**20**
< 30	30	Other	21
30–44	41		
≥ 45	29	**6 – job search**	
		Actively engaged	72
3 – occupational		Not actively engaged	28
category			
Self-employed	3	**7 – receiving benefit**	
Senior management and		Unemployed 1–2 years	
intermediate occupations	8	men	64
Administrative personnel	17	women	52
Skilled manual workers	20	Unemployed ≥ 2 years	
Unskilled manual		men	54
/non-manual workers	45	women	31
Other	7		

4 – educational grade	
I to IV	10
V	33
VI and V [a]	56
Other	1

Source: Compiled by Odile Benoît-Guilbot from INSEE (1989) survey on
employment

CHAPTER 3

FEDERAL REPUBLIC OF GERMANY: CHANGE AND DIVERSITY

Helmut Rudolph

Mid-1991 saw attention in Germany entirely focused on the course of employment in the new Länder of the ex-GDR. By the end of July 1991 there were 1.05 million unemployed, representing an unemployment rate of 12.1 per cent. For the close of the year a figure of nearly 2 million was forecast for the new Länder alone. This dramatic development masks the fact that at the end of 1991 there were still 1.7 million in the West Germany Länder, a figure regarded in the 1970s as socially and politically unacceptable. True some progress has been achieved in the last two years or so; yet from 1983 unemployment increased by 2.1 million. Why then has the unemployment rate taken so long to fall and how far has it failed to keep pace with employment?

Now as then there are more than half a million long-term unemployed who, even given the current favourable situation of the labour market, have little chance of finding a job. Added competition has come with long-distance commuters and migrant workers from the new Länder, predicting a further consolidation of long-term unemployment. In the absence of a short-term solution to the structural problems in the east of the Federal Republic, long-term unemployment can only get worse.

This chapter will deal with the structural changes in unemployment and with the consolidation of long-term unemployment in particular, limiting itself to the territory of the former Federal Republic of Germany, for in the planned economy of the ex-GDR unemployment did not officially exist.

The labour market in the 1980s

The second oil shock of 1980–81 led to a recession in the Federal Republic as elsewhere. Between 1980 and 1983 the number of people

Table 3.1
Labour market since 1980

		1980	1985	1990
Total employed	(. 000)	26980	26489	28423
Unemployed	(. 000)	889	2304	1883
L-T unemployed	(. 000)	106	666	513
Unemployment rate	(%)	3,8	9,3	7,2
Mean duration		15,4	32,9	27,5
of unemployment	(weeks)			
Risk of entering	(%)	12,8	14,7	13,6
unemployment				
L-T unempl. rate	(%)	12,9	31,0	29,7
" " 1–2 yrs	(%)	7,8	16,9	13,8
" " > 2 yrs	(%)	5,1	14,1	15,9

at work dropped by 730,000, while the total working population increased by about 370,000 because of increased numbers of school-leavers entering the labour and training market (see Table 3.1).

Recorded unemployment rose from 889,000 to 2.258 million, a figure that varied little after 1983. Only in 1989 did it show an appreciable drop of 200,000, falling below the 2 million mark in 1990 (1.88 million). The figure 1.6 million registered unemployed is forecast for 1991. The relative stability in the number of unemployed should not mask the significance of activity in the labour market over the same period. Employment grew without interruption from 1984 onwards, representing an increase of 2.1 million in the six years ending in 1990.

The growth in employment was accompanied by rapid structural change, the industrial sector lost some of its relative importance to the services sector, which had a disproportionate growth rate. The share of the secondary sector in overall employment fell back from 51.6 per cent to 46.8 per cent; that of the tertiary sector moved up from 47.3 per cent to 52.2 per cent. The rapid growth of the services sector co-incided with a substantial number of new – often part-time – women's jobs. Between 1980 and 1990 the number working part time and covered by social security rose by 32 per cent or roughly 500,000.

At the beginning of the 1980s school-leavers represented the bulge and competition for jobs and apprenticeship schemes was severe. In the second half of the 1980s the flood of migration from Eastern Europe had to be absorbed. Between 1987 and 1990 1.05 million, roughly half of them of working age, came to the Federal Republic. Thus, in ten years, from 1979 to 1989, the working population grew by almost 2.9 million, the increase in the age group from 15 to 65 counting for

2.25 million, the increased proportion of women in the working population for 924,000, with longer training and earlier retirement reducing
the overall figure by 290,000.

The employment rate of men in the labour force went down from
84.4 per cent to 81.8 per cent, that of women up from 50.2 per cent to
56.2 per cent. Unemployment among young people, which made career
prospects difficult at the start of the 1980s, fell substantially in the course
of time, while today the relatively elderly if excluded from employment
are covered by social security.

Unemployment has held up in spite of the growth in employment
because of the overall imbalance between supply and demand for
labour. Analysis will focus on mechanisms for selecting and apportion-
ing the unemployed, changes in their make-up during the period and
their effects on the structure of long-term unemployment.

The mechanisms of selection

The structures of unemployment are the result of social forces and
multiple mechanisms of selection. Unemployment can be measured
by two of these components: the risk of entry into unemployment,[1]
and the risk of remanence.[2] Taken together these two components
determine the rate of unemployment (i.e. the overall risk of unemployment).

Table 3.2 gives the level and break down of unemployment as risk
of entry and risk of remanence. It shows that the rise in unemployment
in 1981–3 is linked firstly with a marked increase in the risk of entry
and that the risk of remanence rises only after a certain time. Then the
risk of remanence continues to increase while the risk of entry is already
dropping. So the rate of unemployment continued to increase solely
because the length of unemployment was protracted with a decreasing
number of people affected: diminishing risk of entry, increasing risk of
remanence, leading to an increase in long-term unemployment.

The changing pattern in the risk of becoming unemployed was
virtually identical for men and women. Hence the higher rate of unemployment in the case of women is explained more by duration than
by a higher level of risk of entry.

The increase in the risk of remanence, and so the concentration of
unemployment on the long-term unemployed, is evinced by an analysis
of the duration of spells of unemployment. For a given group of unemployed the corresponding volume of unemployment[3] is calculated.
The proportion of the overall volume of unemployment of the 10 per

Table 3.2
Breakdown of unemployment rate

	1983			1990		
	Unem-ployment rate	Dur-ation	Risk of entry	Unem-ployment rate	Dur-ation	Risk of entry
Under 20	9,0	5,5	19,6	4,0	3,1	15,5
20–24	12,1	6,4	22,7	5,5	3,7	17,8
25–34	9,9	7,3	16,3	6,6	5,6	14,1
35–44	6,3	7,5	10,1	5,5	7,0	9,4
45–54	6,1	8,0	9,2	5,6	9,6	7,0
55–59	10,1	10,0	12,1	13,8	18,9	8,8
60–64	10,1	16,0	7,6	12,4	19,1	7,8
Total	8,5	7,2	14,2	6,4	6,7	11,5

cent longest unemployed rose from 31.8 per cent to 42.8 per cent between 1983 and 1990.

Structure of long-term unemployment

During 1990 job centres registered an average of 1.88 million unemployed of whom 29.7 per cent or 513,400 had been unemployed for more than a year and 15.9 per cent for two years or more.[4]

Age

Age is the most decisive variable in the composition of long-term unemployment. It is also in relation to age that the most significant changes have occurred in the course of the 1980s. Between 1983 and 1990 the place of under 25s in overall unemployment fell by almost half (29 per cent to 16 per cent), while that of the over 50s climbed dramatically from 17 per cent to 30 per cent, in spite of easier access to retirement. Young people saw their risk of entry and risk of remanence fall considerably, while with the oldest category the risk of remanence increased considerably in spite of a low risk of entry. These changes are reflected in the long-term unemployment figures.

Thus those under 25 represent only 3.2 per cent of the long-term unemployed, whereas more than half of them (53 per cent) are over 50. The longer the duration of unemployment, the more the oldest category are affected. High unemployment among the young at the start of the 1980s was due to economic recession coinciding with large numbers of school-leavers. At the time, industry took on labour sparingly. Structural changes resulted in the disappearance of numerous jobs, especially in industry. Those with jobs thought twice about changing firms since their employers provided them with a certain degree of security. In these conditions young people completing school or training often found that access to the labour market involved a spell of unemployment. On the other hand, the older wage earners at the time enjoyed a degree of legal protection against being made redundant, at least so long as the firm employing them remained active. Labour market policy at the time was directed towards developing apprenticeship schemes within the firm. In collaboration with employers, the Chancellor promulgated a 'Guarantee of the Right to Vocational Training'. The injunction at the time was to build up reserves of skills. Training programmes aimed at preparing young people for working life, helped relieve the waiting and were a means of giving them an incentive for a career as well as of assimilating them socially.

At the same time, efforts were made to facilitate early retirement for the older category of wage earners, more particularly in major industrial sectors bearing the full impact of the structural crisis. For example, in coal mining, steel or shipbuilding, 'welfare plans' helped to contain massive redundancies by negotiating conditions. Such plans enabled as many as possible of the younger wage earners to keep their jobs; new blood with higher average skills and at a lower cost enabled firms to finance severance pay and supplementary retirement awards or unemployment benefit.

The entire policy was boosted by agreements, negotiated between unions and management, in the matter of early retirement; also by compensatory payments from job centres to firms when they took on someone unemployed in place of an older worker. The right to unemployment benefit was extended from 1 year to 32 months in the case of older workers who, even at 58, had the choice of going back to work; nevertheless, from 60 onwards proof of 1 year's unemployment was sufficient to gain access to full retirement. So for a large number of older wage earners unemployment became a waiting period for retirement without loss of social security benefits.

Qualification

The lack of technical training invariably and substantially heightens the risk of being unemployed. The risk of 'entry' for wage earners without qualifications is more than double the risk for those who have completed a technical training course. The unemployment rate for unskilled workers even in 1990 was 11.7 per cent as against 6.6 per cent in the case of skilled.

Since the tasks required of unskilled workers are also the ones that are likely to be the most physically tiring, the risk of remaining unemployed for those lacking basic skills depends also on age and state of health; those who are relatively old and untrained are therefore the most threatened by long-term unemployment. This being so, it is at first glance surprising that the proportion of unskilled in overall unemployment moved down from 54 per cent in 1980 to 46.8 per cent in 1990. This is explained by a generational change. The older ones, those who had not been able to have any systematic training before and during the war gave way to younger, better trained generations. At the same time the decline in the numbers of school-leavers had its effect on the number of young people who found themselves unemployed before they had had any technical training.

The proportion of unemployed without training increases with the length of unemployment. Those with fewer qualifications represent 44 per cent of those unemployed for under a year and 60.7 per cent of those unemployed for more than 4 years. In 1990 the unskilled counted for 53 per cent in the volume of unemployment.

Generally speaking, the rate of unemployment decreases when the level of technical training rises. In the middle of the 1980s unemployment prevailing among wage earners was first and foremost accounted for by the closing of outlets in certain specific fields. For instance, the drop in the numbers of schoolchildren forced the government to call a halt to the recruitment of teachers. The development of welfare posts and openings in the arts came up against budgetary restraint in the civil service. Scores of young people, who at the beginning of the 1980s had undertaken apprenticeships in occupations where prospects and needs had been poorly assessed, found themselves unemployed.

In-house training and steps to implement retraining are in this respect essential components of an active labour market policy. In 1990 the BA (Bundesanstalt für Arbeit, Federal Employment Bureau) provided 6.400.000 DM, thus allowing 575,000, of whom two thirds were unemployed and a quarter without technical training, to attend schemes financed by the Bureau. The 'Skills Offensive' launched in 1987 aimed among other things to reduce the mismatch between the skills demanded on the labour market and those that many unemployed found no call for. Of those who completed the training courses, 45 per cent found a job.

State of health

A quarter of unemployed in 1990 showed evidence of poor health. The figure was 32 per cent in 1980, but the redundancies caused by the recession and higher unemployment among young people brought it down to under 20 per cent in 1983, before the mechanisms for selection raised it again to the present level. For those in poor health the risk of long-term unemployment is particularly high, 40 per cent of this category presenting such problems. Clearly the difficulties of being taken on increase with age. Selection mechanisms have led to an over-representation of unemployed for health reasons. Further, surveys have shown that health problems occur when unemployment persists (Brinkmann and Potthoff, 1983; Brinkmann 1984). Loss of employment, with its accompanying financial problems and a diminished personal role, engenders psychological and social difficulties both for the unemployed and their families (Hess *et al.*, 1991).

Women

On average, the relative place of long-term unemployment is roughly the same for women (29 per cent) as for men (30 per cent). But if variables such as age, degree of skill, full-time or part-time job search are kept constant, it is noticeable that female rates of long-term unemployment are higher in almost every category. Indeed a representation by age-groups, more favourable to women, evens out on average the specific divergences in the different categories.

In short, long-term unemployment is increasingly focused on older age groups – the critical age at which unemployment becomes more acute has dropped to 45 – and those affected by ill-health. Among young people, apart from a fringe group, long-term unemployment as a problem has disappeared and has slightly less impact on those with low skills.

Economic sectors

Surprisingly, study of the relationship between structural changes in the economy and long-term unemployment has been neglected. True a third of long-term unemployed were not working before registering as unemployed, hence cannot be linked to one sector or another. Generally speaking, the proportion of long-term unemployed among wage-earners in the industrial sector is higher than for the services sector. Among those unemployed in branches that experienced significant redundancy in the 1980s – mining, steel, shipbuilding, textiles and construction – long-term unemployment is particularly high. In the mining and steel industries it reaches over 60 per cent in spite of welfare plans which frequently accompany redundancy.

Even so, overall the proportion of long-term unemployed who come from these branches is fairly slight. Jobs in the metallurgical industry count for 14 per cent here. Occupations demanding lower skills such as warehousing, transport and dispatching also account for roughly 14 per cent of long-term unemployment. Despite the structural changes that favour office and service occupations, these account variously for 11 per cent and nearly 9 per cent (business employees), 11.4 per cent of long-term unemployment relating to commerce, which represents 13.5 per cent of the labour force, although figures for employment here have been in line with the general average over recent years.

Population changes account for a considerable part of unemployment. Structural changes in production have also been held responsible for long-term unemployment, but the fact that it is widely spread across all branches and occupations seems to rule this out. Even so the transformation of production entails movement within long-term unemployment. A survey carried out in Bremen showed that a cutback of shipyard workers led to a corresponding increase in unemployment in the area, but that a quarter of those laid off found another job without facing unemployment; and that, within a year, 60 per cent of them were back in other jobs. Being highly qualified, they rapidly found work in other branches. At the same time, the labour market contracted for other categories of unemployed, sometimes in the same occupation. Public response to the closing of the shipyards and the wave of sympathy enjoyed by those who had formerly worked there and been made redundant apparently saved them from the ignominy of unemployment. They would seem to have been treated as a special case while others became unemployed in their stead, one might conclude (Heseler, 1990).

Recurrent unemployment, cumulative unemployment and long-term unemployment

The official definition of long-term unemployment relates to the last continuous period of registration at the Federal Employment Bureau (BA). If this is broken into by short-term spells of work, bouts of sick leave, moving house or periods of training, the duration of unemploy-

ment returns to zero. Thereby the method of reckoning unemployment spells statistically underestimates the real length of long-term unemployment.
According to poll surveys, long-term unemployment represents 42.3 per cent whereas BA statistics put it at 32.6 per cent. In the case of very long-term unemployment the official figure is markedly minimised. The social dimension of unemployment, such as it is experienced subjectively by those concerned, differs widely from the measures effected according to the legal criteria of registration. Periods of training or sickness are felt by those concerned to be an integral part of their unemployment. Moreover, since 1986 unemployed over 58 can claim unemployment benefit even if they declare themselves unwilling to go back to working for a wage; in which case, they must retire as soon as they can, normally at 60, and are no longer registered as unemployed. To date, roughly 60,000 people have taken this option.

Table 3.3
Proportion of long-term unemployment (as %)
according to BA statistics and surveys

	Statistics 1990	BA 1988	Microcensus 1988	Infratest 1988	OECD 1989
Unempl. over					
1 year	29,7	32,6	42,3	43	49,0
2 years	15,9	16,5	27,3	26	
3 years	9,8	9,9			
4 years	6,4	6,3			

Table 3.4
Recurrent unemployment
over the period 1977–1986

Number of spells	Persons Millions	Persons %	Volume %
1	6,665	54,2	35,8
2	2,803	22,7	23,7
3	1,307	10,6	15,0
4	0,664	5,4	9,4
> 4	0,853	6,9	16,1
Total	12,292	100,0	100,0

Source: Reproduced from Karr and John, 1989, 11–12

The underestimation of long-term unemployment is also open to adjustment by studying recurrent unemployment, where spells of job loss are broken by brief exits from registration or by temporary jobs. Surveys reveal that, if recurrent unemployment is taken into account, the burden of unemployment can appear for some to be much more oppressive than the length of the last spell of unemployment allows. Between 1977 and 1986 (Karr and John, 1989) it was calculated that 12.3 million different people sustained 24.4 million spells of registered unemployment. This points to an average recurrent spell of 1.98 and an average length of unemployment of 20.3 weeks per spell and 40.2 weeks per individual. Certainly the period under observation covers very different situations in the labour market; 54.2 per cent experienced a single period of unemployment representing only 35.8 per cent of the total volume, while 6.9 per cent had been unemployed more than four times and represented 16.1 per cent of the volume.

The impact of recurrence on the length of unemployment is clearly visible. In a survey conducted in 1989, 23 per cent of those unemployed declared they had been unemployed several times in the course of the previous five years. Some unemployed, who at the time of the survey had been unemployed for less than a year, on average for 6.5 months, had a cumulative length of unemployment amounting to 14 months or more (Infratest, 1989). The results of the different surveys concur: men, manual workers, people of low skills, people in seasonal employment, together with young people are at higher risk from recurrent unemployment.

Types of passage through unemployment

During the 1980s unemployment took on a different posture in the turnover of the workforce in the labour market. In the light of the situation before and after employment (i.e. having an occupation (OCC) or not having an occupation (NOCC)), four types of experiencing unemployment can be distinguished:

Type	Entry	Exit
1	OCC	OCC
2	NOCC	OCC
3	OCC	NOCC
4	NOCC	NOCC

For 1983 and 1990 all exits from unemployment recorded during a survey conducted over two weeks were classed under these four types.

Table 3.5

Types of passage through unemployment 1983–1990

| | | Situation after unemployment | |
		Working	Non-working

Situation before unemployment	Working	Type 1 : OCC–OCC
		
		1983 Cases 62.5%
		      Duration 163
		      Volume 55.3%
		
		1990 Cases 37.2%
		      Duration 150
		      Volume 27.7%
			Type 3 : OCC–NOCC
			
			1983 Cases 24.01%
			      Duration 242
			      Volume 29.6%
			
			1990 Cases 21.4%
			      Duration 321
			      Volume 34.0%

	Non-working	Type 2 : NOCC–OCC
		
		1983 Cases 6.8%
		      Duration 181
		      Volume 6.4%
		
		1990 Cases 16.5%
		      Duration 149
		      Volume 12.2%
			Type 4 : NOCC–NOCC
			
			1983 Cases 6.6%
			      Duration 251
			      Volume 8.8%
			
			1990 Cases 24.8%
			      Duration 214
			      Volume 26.3%

Source: Calculations based on BA statistics, 1983 and 1990

Median duration was calculated and the weighting of each case with its length of unemployment made it possible to obtain the volume of cumulative unemployment for those exiting. Computation of the cumulative volume for the four types of experience provides results that are remarkable insofar as the course of unemployment between 1983 and 1990 is concerned.

In 1983 62.5 per cent of the unemployment spells were of Type 1 OCC–OCC; median duration of unemployment for this group was 163 days and formed 55.3 per cent of the volume of unemployment. In 1990 Type 1 cases counted for no more than 37.2 per cent, median duration had fallen to 150 days and the proportion of volume of unemployment between two jobs had dropped appreciably.

Conversely, the number of Type 2 cases NOCC–OCC showed a rise. The period of unemployment here corresponds to a process of becoming integrated or reintegrated after time out of employment. On average the length of these spells of unemployment was exactly the same as for the first group. The other two types (OCC–NOCC and NOCC–NOCC), which correspond, in part, to temporary exclusion from the labour market, with 60 per cent for 1990, took on distinctly greater significance in volume. Certainly in the 1980s unemployment was frequently transformed into a period of waiting for retirement.

'Bogus unemployment'

The surprising fact that the number of jobs increases at the same time as unemployment has led in certain quarters to the unemployed being blamed for their failure to be available for work while firms are unable to satisfy their own labour needs in quantity and in quality. The term 'bogus unemployed' (Rosenbladt, 1991) designates unemployed who are not really job-seekers. A distinction has to be made between benefit abuse and situations where unemployment provides a legal status conferring welfare rights. In the course of moving from employment to non-employment, being registered as unemployed gives legal right to an income, to social security, to retirement benefit or to welfare allowances. According to the Infratest survey, 1989, 18 per cent of those unemployed are in this situation (16 per cent after being unemployed for three years): 10 per cent gave notice of taking retirement in the near future, 5 per cent of starting a training course, 2 per cent of going on maternal leave and 1 per cent of enlisting in the army. Nearly half of these temporarily unemployed said they were not seeking work at the time of the survey. They represented two thirds of the unemployed not actively seeking work; nor were they all in receipt of benefit. Among long-term unemployed the safeguard of welfare rights becomes an increasingly important reason to maintain registration.

The proportion of unemployed who cheat is difficult to calculate. According to the BA services, 21 per cent of unemployed, including some who are registered in order to keep up their welfare rights, are not seriously concerned with returning to work; 94 per cent had managed to find a new job and 82 per cent of those who had been unemployed for over three years had carried their own job search independently of the BA services. A third of those unemployed and almost half the long-term unemployed had made over ten applications to firms, very often without receiving any reply. Bogus unemployment would seem then to represent only a very small portion of registered unemployed. Refusal of job offers does not always signify unreadiness to work, but more often consciousness on the part of the unemployed that what is offered is unsuited to their abilities. This explains the fact that a more than average number of unemployed who had previously turned down jobs found employment while the survey was being conducted.

Standard of living of those unemployed

The unemployed are entitled to unemployment benefit Arbeitslosengeld, ALG), when they have worked for at least one year during the three years preceding unemployment. The duration of this benefit payment depends in a ratio of two to one on the length of time worked. Up to age 41 it is paid for a maximum period of 1 year, increasing with age and length of employment to reach 32 months at 54. The amount of benefit is 63 per cent of the last net wage after tax, about 68 per cent with dependent children. After this benefit expires, an unemployment aid payment (Arbeitslosenhilfe, ALHI) is paid for an unlimited time, according to need; it represents 56 per cent (or 58 per cent where there are children) of the last net wage. Any other income received by the household is taken into account.

At the start of unemployment about three-quarters of those unemployed receive benefit or aid. As benefit may end before unemployment does, 66 per cent only of the long-term unemployed received benefit or aid in 1990.

Unemployment benefit represents about 36 per cent of family income and is often not enough to protect the unemployed from serious financial worries. According to surveys, allowances and unemployment aid are the main source of income only for a third of families where one member or more is unemployed; for 22 per cent of families they are the only source of income. In the case of a further third, allowances represent up to 60 per cent of income, while the third remaining receive no allowance.

About a third of the unemployed report that they are in financial difficulties. With a ten-year interval this proportion has not increased, but their number in absolute terms has doubled simply because unemployment has increased. The majority manage, thanks to other sources of income, by making sacrifices. Unemployed males, married and fathers, who are the sole earners, and single males not living with their parents, face the worst financial problems. In addition to money received by way of unemployment benefit and aid, retirement or support payment as well as allowances from other social insurance funds (welfare benefit, housing benefit, family and maternity allowances) supplement household incomes. The older employed who are close to retirement and married women whose husbands enjoy an income are better off financially. According to criteria acknowledged to be objective, 38 per cent of the unemployed are below the poverty threshold. They receive unemployment or welfare aid, the obtaining of which depends on assessment of income.

According to another survey (Brinkmann *et al.*, 1991), in September 1989 17 per cent of unemployed depended wholly or in part on welfare benefit to maintain their families. This corresponds to about 310,000 unemployed (and 286,000 households). In 1985 this figure was only 13 per cent – hence poverty among the unemployed has risen. According to welfare agency records, in the course of 1980 80,000 households received welfare payment through loss of employment. During 1989 476,000 households (including people looking for their first job) applied to welfare agencies because of unemployment. They included a third needing continuous aid, the majority of them long-term unemployed or those with unemployment recurring over the preceding three years.

Financial difficulties show little increase as unemployment persists (Rosenbladt, 1991). They come to have a significant effect only after three years, forcing those concerned to turn to welfare aid; they are the cause of getting behind with monthly instalment payments (15 per cent), insurance payments (12 per cent), savings schemes (10 per cent) and rent (10 per cent).

Conclusion

In summing up, it has to be recognised that the economic position of the unemployed worsened during the 1980s, except for middle-aged unemployed who had held a stable job for more than four years. At the start of the period there was a phase when the right to benefit was reduced. Unemployed who had worked fewer than six months and students who had taken examinations were not indemnified; also the ratio between length of employment and period of compensation was lowered from two to one to three to one. Further, the replacement rate for unemployed without children was reduced from 68 per cent to 63 per cent of net wage after tax.[6] On the other hand, for the unemployed of over 42 the ratio duration of employment/duration of compensation has been restored to 2 to 1, and the period of compensation increased from 12 to 15–32 months.

With long-term unemployment and the increase in the number of people searching for a job without having worked during the previous three years (women following the crucial period of children's schooling, migrant workers of German stock from Eastern Europe), the proportion of unemployed who are less well indemnified has increased. If today the proportion of unemployed receiving compensation (66 per cent) is slightly higher than it was in 1980, the ratio between those who receive benefit and those who receive aid has shifted from 5 to 1 to 2 to 1. Moreover the proportion of unemployed resorting to welfare aid increased from 10.3 per cent in 1980 to 13.1 per cent in 1989, equivalent to a multiplication by 3.5 in absolute terms.

In 1989 the Federal Government set up a special programme to fight long-term unemployment. Provision was made for an injection of 1.5 billion DM between then and the end of 1991, in the form of subsidies capable of realising up to 80 per cent of wage payments, so enabling up to 70,000 unemployed to secure wage employment on open-ended contract. The sum of 50 million DM was put at the disposal of eight employment agencies with the aim of trying out new methods of long-term integration by combining forms of aid originating from the BA, municipalities, the Länder and the EU. The programme was supplemented by projects whose administrative, investment and staffing costs are financed to an overall limit of an extra 490 million marks. Hence, various initiatives have made it possible to combine occupational activity, training and welfare assistance (for example, counselling households who have got into debt). By the end of 1990 provision had been made for 13,000 jobs for the long-term unemployed and others who were particularly difficult to place.

Notes

1. Measured by the number of entries in relation to the total labour force (actively employed plus unemployed).
2. Duration of entire spell of unemployment. This measurement is more reliable than duration of current spell and presupposes longitudinal findings.
3. The distinction has to be made between persons unemployed and 'volume of unemployment', total non-working time on account of unemployment. The volume of unemployment of a person unemployed for twelve months is equal to that of twelve unemployed people each spending one month in unemployment.
4. These figures are lower than those supplied in the introduction. They represent registrations at job centres and are, for most countries, lower than those that emerge from national labour force surveys made use of by OECD and SOEC.
5. Study is based on results of the survey 'Job search, occupational mobility and social situation in regard to the unemployed', undertaken by the Federal

Ministry of Labour and in which unemployed persons, employment agents and industrialists took part. See BMA, 1990; Infratest, 1989.

6. A parliamentary bill for 1994 aims to reduce rates of ALG and ALHI benefit, with the intention of limiting ALHI benefit to two years.

CHAPTER 4

ITALY – A LONG WAIT IN THE SHELTER OF THE FAMILY AND SAFEGUARDS FROM THE STATE

Emilio Reyneri

The belated discovery

During the early 1990s in Italy six out of ten unemployed have been engaged in job searching for more than twelve months; ten years ago there were fewer than three. This level of long-term unemployment, the highest in Europe apart from Belgium, has led neither to research nor to a political strategy. The reasons put forward to account for unemployment on this scale, which has been rising since 1974, cover the difficult transition between school and work, the novel impact of the influx of women into the labour market and the factor of underdevelopment in the Mezzogiorno (south).

The growth of long-term unemployment, coinciding with the increase in overall unemployment, may appear natural. Yet in every country in Europe long-term unemployment focused attention, when it became evident that its rate continued to increase while the rate of overall unemployment remained stable or even fell. In Italy the unemployment rate has not risen since 1987 and has even dropped in the Centre-North. It is in relation to this region and only recently that long-term unemployment has begun to pose a problem.

Duration of unemployment is linked to variations in overall unemployment. The stock of those who are seeking work increases when the inflow into unemployment over the year is greater than the outflow (whether for reasons of finding work or of abandoning the job search). But the 'new entrants' who remain unemployed become long-term unemployed the following year. The percentage of long-term unemployed would not increase if the outflow from unemployment during year t was equal to the inflow during year $t–1$. This condition, which presupposes a stable level of unemployment, is essential, but not sufficient, for if the first entrants were also the first leavers, the number of long-term unemployed would still go on growing. It is clear however that a marked growth in overall unemployment leads to a growth in long-term unemployment.

On the political side, it is urgent to reduce the overall volume of unemployment and to respond to pressure from the strongest and best organised of the unemployed, among whom the unemployed who have been without work for a long time, and who are weaker and more marginal, are not to be found; this is the more urgent since it may well be that the measures in favour of the long-term unemployed have the perverse effect of not reducing overall unemployment. (See Sibille, 1989: 30–31.)

Italian anomalies

In 1987 the overall unemployment rate in Italy conformed to the average in Europe (10.7 per cent); its composition continues to be distinctive compared to that of other European countries (see Table 4.1) and unemployment is still higher for women and young people and substantially less high for adult men. In the case of adult men it is virtually equal to half the European average (i.e. 5.6 per cent) and the difference is still greater for married men (2.5 per cent). Even in the Mezzogiorno, where the overall unemployment rate is nearly three-quarters higher than the European average, in the case of married men the figure is lower than 5 per cent; and male unemployed who have lost their jobs represent only 10 per cent as against 46 per cent.

We shall single out three representative groups of unemployed in Italy. First, young people, who after leaving school may spend a long time searching for a stable regular job without needing to take what is on offer, simply because they live at home, are kept by their parents and often, particularly in the Centre-North, make do with small jobs. Second, adult married women, in no special hurry to find work, since it has to fit in with their obligations to the family. Third, a much less numerous group, the unemployed who have lost their jobs. These are adult men (particularly in the Mezzogiorno where unemployment is endemic), who live from work in the black economy, from state grants to agriculture or on disability benefits, for genuine or less than genuine reasons (the number of cases of disability is remarkably high).

On the other hand, the type of unemployment that, in other European countries, has directed attention to the question of long-term unemployment – manual workers driven out in the course of restructuring by large firms where they have worked for a number of years – is

Table 4.1

Extent of long-term unemployment in Italy 1977–1989
(as % of overall unemployment)

	ITALIE		MEZZOGIORNO		CENTRE-NORTH		EMILIA-ROMAGNA	
	1977	1989	1978	1988	1978	1988	1981	1989
Men	29,6	56,8	30,5	59,8	26,9	44,7	16,1	29,2
Women	27,7	59,7	33,8	62,3	30,2	53,0	25,0	39,3
Total	27,4	58,5	32,2	61,2	28,8	50,0	22,2	36,5
Seeking first job	32,8	67,5	37,8	71,3	31,3	56,3	25,5	48,3
Seeking following loss	18,4	31,7	13,4	28,6	23,8	33,0	12,5	22,2
Other unemployed	23,1	59,9	30,2	61,2	26,7	54,0	25,0	38,1

Source: Reproduced from Istat, *Labour force surveys*

uncommon in Italy. Being advanced in years and having skills that are no longer required, such workers tend to remain unemployed for a long time and, since as often as not they are the head a household, their economic and social position can give cause for anxiety.

Industrial reorganisation eliminated several hundred thousand jobs without leading to an increase in unemployment, because workers thus affected instead of being made redundant fell back on the Cassa integrazione guadagni (CIG), a fund financed by the state which compensates for loss of earnings to nearly 90 per cent and theoretically for an indeterminate period of time.[1]

Workers who were surplus due to reorganisation by large firms were not considered to be unemployed. Yet for several years the volume of cassa-integrati (those enjoying these benefits) represented between two-thirds and three-quarters of the volume of unemployed who had lost their jobs. Had the cassa-integrati been counted as unemployed, the structure of unemployment in Italy would as a result have been rather more close to that of other European countries[2]. For instance, the percentage of unemployed seeking work after loss of employment might have risen to 17 per cent, with heads of households at 23 per cent. However the differences in relation to European averages are still too great to be explained solely in terms of institutional or statistical causes.

The Italian anomaly becomes more pronounced

Of the total number of unemployed 47 per cent are young people who have spent over a year looking for a first job, compared with a European average of 18 per cent. Against this, fewer than 4 per cent are adults engaged in searching for a new job for more than a year, compared with a European average of more than 17 per cent. In Italy the 'long wait' refers essentially to women and young people on the look out for a first job.

Between 1977 and 1989, for which period figures are roughly comparable,[3] the volume of those who spent more than twelve months in job-searching tripled whereas the figure for overall unemployment merely doubled. Virtually the whole increase in unemployment was due to the spectacular rise in long-term unemployed and from 27 per cent their proportion has risen to exceed 58 per cent. However, pronounced differences according to sex and circumstances of job-search are to be noted (see Table 4.1). The percentage of long-term unemployed is not only lower among unemployed who have lost their jobs, its increase is also less conspicuous (from 18 per cent to 31 per cent). For those who have had experience of working and who are actively engaged in trying to find another job, the forms of exclusion induced by long stretches of fruitless job-searching meet with little favour, hence the rise here has been less pronounced of late. Adults who have already achieved entry into the 'fortress of employment' shut the gates on young people and on women.

Conversely, among those seeking their first job the percentage of long-term unemployed, which was already much higher, doubled between 1977 and 1989 (33 per cent to 67 per cent). The rise was also much more pronounced among 'other persons unemployed', for the most part housewives, students and pensioners who declared they were job-searching, albeit not particularly strenuously; with women nevertheless the percentage of long-term unemployed is six to ten points higher than with men. Women here can remain unemployed for a long time, without really applying themselves to job-seeking since, whether they like to or not, they put their family responsibilities foremost; students or pensioners are simply waiting to seize an opportunity when it turns up.

However in recent years, the percentage of young people has dropped from 80 per cent to 73 per cent, that of those seeking a first job from 68 per cent to 63 per cent, while that of adults with work experience is slightly higher. The fact that the trend has had no impact on the gender ratio shows that even among adults with work experience, women long-term unemployed still form the largest number. This situation, a new one for Italy where most adult women were 'becoming disheartened' and turning their backs on the labour market, is much more widespread in the Centre-North, where alongside the girl trying for her first job a new figure in long-term unemployment is now apparent – the adult woman, who while considering herself first and foremost as a housewife, is manifesting an ill-defined desire to find a job.

Trends and differences in long-term unemployment in the 'several Italies'

The level, the dynamic and the structure of unemployment are entirely distinct in the Centre-North and in the Mezzogiorno. Taking Italy as a whole, the overall volume of unemployment virtually doubled between 1978 and 1989, whereas in the Centre-North the increase was barely 40 per cent; and this relatively lower overall unemployment rate was accompanied by an equally lower percentage of long-term unemployment. But when unemployment began to fall, no change followed in the long-term unemployment percentage, which tends to confirm the serious problems encountered by the long-term unemployed, even when better conditions are prevailing in the labour market.

In the Mezzogiorno unemployment is considerably higher than the national average and it has increased much more rapidly. As regards long-term unemployment one can talk in terms of an explosion, since the figures for 1988 were five times higher than for 1978. The percentage of long-term unemployed, already higher than the national average, rose from 32 per cent to 61 per cent, but contrary to what occurred in the Centre-North, this percentage is less high so far as women who have lost their job are concerned, because unemployed adult women become more readily disheartened and exit sooner from the labour market. Long-term unemployment hits young people seeking a first job and women especially, even so adult men who have lost their jobs have become more numerous over recent years and pose serious social problems. It should be borne in mind that the unemployment rate of married men has never, even in the Mezzogiorno, risen above 6 per cent.

By way of contrast, let us take a look at the case of Emilia-Romagna, one of the richest regions, where the overall rate of unemployment (under 5 per cent) verges on full employment and where the long-term unemployment percentage, in the order of 40 per cent between 1985 and 1987, fell to 36 per cent in 1989. Over the same period, the average for the Centre-North remained constant at slightly above 50 per cent and the national average continued to increase. Emilia-Romagna anticipated a gradual lowering in the overall unemployment rate, which characterised every region in the Centre-North in 1985, while long-term unemployment went on growing. It began to fall the following year, but it was two years more before its percentage came down. From this it can be seen that long-term unemployment responds weakly and protractedly to improved conditions in the labour market. It seems evident that the long-term unemployed have to face greater difficulties, even when there is a marked recovery in the demand for labour and in a region until then little affected.

Among long-term unemployed, the proportion of women is higher than in the Centre-North regions and that of young people much less so (young men seeking a first job count for close on 10 per cent against an average of 20 per cent for the Centre-North). The conclusion would seem to be that when unemployment drops, long-term unemployment becomes concentrated on the weaker group, who with competition becoming more acute tend to abandon the search for employment.

Recent sociological research[4] throws further light on the characteristics of the long-term unemployed in conditions of full employment. Half the unemployed women and 31 per cent of the men are married, the difference due in part to population factors but clearly underlining that those who pursue the search for regular stable employment longest are those with fewer financial commitments (i.e. married women, whose husbands are nearly always working, and unmarried men). Indeed, the long-term unemployment rate for married men – those who face the strongest pressure to stay at work – is only 8 per cent as against 38 per cent for married women and 40 per cent for unmarried men of under 30, almost all of them living with parents who are working. Long-term unemployment fails to reach more than 14 per cent of unmarried men over 30, and only a small minority of long-term unemployed live alone without family support. A fairly high percentage of long-term unemployed live in large families but only 4 per cent of women and 19 per cent of men have dependent relatives. In the case of large families, the occupations of other family members enable the long-term unemployed to be kept and carry on indefinitely with the search for employment. Real difficulties rarely develop; if they do, they generally involve older married men with poor schooling. Finally it should be added that in Emilia-Romagna 17 per cent of the long-term unemployed are in reality makeshift workers, hired for seasonal jobs in farming and the tourist trade in the course of the previous twelve months.

Long-term unemployment in Italy: a serious but not acute problem?

In Italy institutional and societal factors afford an explanation of why long-term unemployment has been concentrated in sections of the population able to withstand a long period of waiting without sustaining too much damage, the young living with their families, married women and *cassa-integrati.*

In the cities of the Mezzogiorno, boys and girls who are unemployed dress no differently from their peers who are earning or students, they like the same music and frequent the same clubs. With its somewhat special structure, unemployment in Italy today has lost the high physical profile that once characterised it and that persists only in a few limited enclaves, among small firms struck down in the process of de-industrialisation and outside the province of the CIG

Two recent surveys of poverty[5] in Italy have shown clearly the distinction between unemployment and poverty. Today unemployment is no more than a marginal cause of poverty, compared with predominant factors such as old age and poor health conditions. The poor constitute only 13 per cent of the total of unemployed and the unemployed represent only 5 per cent of the poor. If the vast majority of unemployed people in Italy, even long-term unemployed, are neither poor nor stigmatised in the eyes of the public, it is because they are protected either by their families or by the state-funded CIG.

Finally the last new element, the most flagrant perhaps but the least analysed: the long wait for first employment that now affects boys and girls of average families. With the transition between school and work being difficult, unemployment has spread into the families of office workers, civil servants, tradespeople and teachers for the first time since the 1930s, even if the situation, at the present time, is far less dramatic. This cross-sectional character of long-term unemployment among young people has given rise to significant forms of expression.

It cannot be said that in the 1980s unemployment in Italy had really serious economic consequences on family living conditions, although its duration grew longer and longer. Again one should stress that it applied chiefly to young people or married women. Furthermore during this period employment was still rising, the ratio between those with occupations and the total population being 36.1 per cent in 1977 and 37.4 per cent in 1990. Moreover there was a marked increase in 'double employment' bringing with it extra income into the family. It has been estimated that in 1980 roughly 13 per cent of men employed had another paid job not in agriculture and that in 1986 those holding two or more jobs counted for more than 16 per cent.[6] Possibly many fathers work twice over to enable their sons to sustain the long initial wait for employment.

An appreciation of the situation may well be very different if one considers it from a social point of view. The majority of young people have had to live out a kind of long 'moratorium' with no studying and no regular or lasting work. The consequent risks of real decline in the importance given to the role of work, in the way that young people construct their social identity, become evident. This is the price that Italy has paid to preserve its adult and family men from unemployment. Now the story of how this has happened needs to be addressed.

Insiders versus outsiders and the role of the submerged economy

The contrast between the mass of young people engaged in their first job search and the few adults seeking work takes on the appearance of a conflict between outsiders and insiders, which is without equivalent in other countries. As an explanation the hypothesis has been put forward of a stock of irremovable workers, who enjoy legal and union protection, and hence block access to employment for younger generations. But the image of employment as a 'fortress' does not entirely correspond with reality (see Reyneri, 1989a).

Certainly the CIG allows surplus workers in large firms to present themselves as having an occupation and thus avoid unemployment. But the CIG expanded only after 1980, whereas the practice is older and, above all, analysis of employment flows reveals high mobility between jobs on the part of workers who are employed. It should be added that in Italy the distribution of seasonal jobs in agriculture and the construction and tourist industries allow even temporary wage-earners in these sectors to receive special unemployment benefits, which are in actual fact incorporated into annual earnings. One can visualise a regular pattern of movement into and out of employment, the effect of which would be to reduce the percentage of long-term unemployed among all who have lost their jobs.

If there is indeed a barrier to young people entering the labour market, it resides principally in the fact that the individual who has a job and loses it finds another fairly quickly and easily, while the young face an ordeal of odd-jobbing in order to attain their first stable employment. A number of factors combine to penalise young young school-leavers with no work experience. In the past legislation encouraged firms to give priority recruitment to workers already employed elsewhere enabling them to enjoy complete discretion in the matter of selection, whereas taking on someone unemployed involved reference to a schedule set by state employment agencies. But the most striking factor was the dearth of any technical or vocational training for young people, hence their inability to prepare for the demands of employment. It is not at all improbable that the system of vocational training in Italy is the worst in any industrialised nation, but this is not the place to develop that question.

A complex and sociologically interesting set of circumstances underlies the failure to adjust, in the widest sense, to the demands of employment. It is worth recalling that at the end of the 1960s and for ten years or so the Italian educational system was convulsed by very rapid development in higher education and the adoption of overlax selection procedures as well as by attitudes on the part of students, which were fed by an ideology hostile to industry. Young people leaving higher education believed they would have access to high-level professional positions hitherto assured them, from a time when higher education was still the preserve of a restricted élite. To many of these young people, thanks to financial support from the family and casual jobs, it appeared reasonable to pursue a long-term strategy of waiting for an occupation to come up that conformed to the pattern of aspiration which they and their families had earlier acquired. In any case, firms were very reticent about taking on young people with what they considered excessive pretentions, lacking adaptability, unused to self-restraint and frequently hostile to discipline and the notion of hierarchy.

The situation began to change at the start of the 1980s. Since 1984 work-training contracts not only authorise the recruitment of young people with complete liberty of choice but also provide not inconsiderable grants. Moreover, a good part of the increase in unemployment through loss of jobs is due to the exit from the CIG of workers from large firms who are often older and poorly qualified. Besides there have also been changes in the educational system and in preparation for employment: a slow-but-sure readjustment in the links between educational attainment and what is and what is not seen to be acceptable in the matter of placement. Young people and their families are beginning to accept the idea that vocational qualifications do not allow automatic access to high positions. Added to this, the climate within schools has changed. Indulgence and permissiveness have lived their time and given way afresh to an acceptance of selection and discipline. So it is that both from the point of view of demand and supply the factors which curbed the inflow of young people into the world of employment are gradually losing distinction. The Italian anomaly of youth unemployment, particularly of young people who hold qualifications, is on the way to disappearing, in the Centre-North at least; but it will take some time for the process to work itself through.

The real gap between the Centre-North and the Mezzogiorno remains. The unemployment rate in the Mezzogiorno reached 21 per cent in 1988 as compared with 7 per cent in the regions of the North, and this distinction is more sharply focused with long-term unemployment. For some time several provinces in the Centre-North have been experiencing full employment, whereas disinclination to emigrate persists in the Mezzogiorno despite a continuing rise in unemployment. Internal migration, halted half way through the 1970s, has not resumed in spite of the growing disparity between the regional employment markets. The absence of mobility where unemployed from the South are concerned may be explained both in terms of demand – difficulties in finding accommodation in towns in the Centre-North, decentralisation affecting productive units – and of supply – the disincentives produced by a combination of social aid policies and the prevalence of irregular working in the Mezzogiorno. With the fall in employment in the larger firms a whole organisational principle that once informed the employment market has disappeared. Indeed the major firms gave regulation to a series of sub-markets, bringing in the building trade and small factories. Their 'blocked' demand was such as to determine waves of migration. Today it is all over. In the Mezzogiorno the underground economy, assisted by state grants, supplies families with an income, which though at a low level provides a means of subsistence. Hence job-searching in the Centre-North loses its attraction; the costs of displacement – financial, social and psychological – are too high.

The recent cultural changes that have taken place in the advancement of women and their role can explain the high proportion of housewives among the long-term unemployed. Traditionally Italy used to be characterised by a low representation of women in the labour market for socioeconomic and cultural reasons. In recent years the situation has changed radically for girls, who by achieving higher academic grades are actively beginning to look for jobs and more and more often manage to find them. On the other hand, it is more ambiguous for adult women who, traditionally and with the position they hold in the cycle of family life, are to a greater extent bound by domestic ties. Most of them are seeking, however idly, for work that is compatible with family constraints (i.e. part-time and within easy distance of home); yet they have seldom had the schooling required.

The well-protected unemployed: strategies employed by the cassa-integrati

The majority of long-term unemployed in Italy are able to remain so and avoid their economic position becoming too serious, because they are young and live with their families or because they are married women; often they contribute to the family income by doing odd jobs. So they are not obliged to accept the first chance of work that comes along. These somewhat precarious filler jobs have a function in making young people more alive to problems and in putting off the final choice of a job. The case of the *cassa-integrati* is hardly different; they too have the guarantee of a fixed benefit to depend on for a virtually unlimited time. In such cases, it is highly likely that the attitudes of the unemployed are dictated less by the pressures of economic need than by strategic considerations and those of individual freedom.

Various studies made of the *cassa-integrati* allow one to fill in the picture of their situation and see their social role in all its complexity. The length of time spent in the CIG and the time of exit depend to a large extent on sex, age, educational attainment and skills but a large number of exit patterns of workers from the CIG cannot be explained in these terms. The first to leave are not always the most apt even if they have no trouble finding an acceptable job. With unemployed having comparable attributes entering the labour market simultaneously, those who are first in the job-search have an advantage over the rest, who may find the demand for labour largely satisfied. Cumulative action on the part of individuals generates a kind of vicious circle which penalises latecomers. This state of affairs is sometimes made worse by a firm's inclination to go for someone with only a short spell in the CIG rather than another who has made use of it for as long as possible, as well as by the loss of morale felt by anyone out of work for a long time. Among those who find a better job more easily two groups can be distinguished: the one 'bright and competitive' (adults who are well-educated and qualified), the other 'adaptable and flexible' (low skills, low educational attainment). The second group makes up for its weaknesses by showing positive readiness for change and high adaptability, which can be seen as 'resolution and preparedness'. On the other hand, for the bright workers from the first group rapid exit from the CIG can sometimes lead to a poor job. Their decision to exit without delay may be explained by their unreadiness to tolerate a situation that they deem to be precarious, but the unreadiness to face uncertainty itself requires explanation. The work ethic of some highly professional workers, who are older and have experience of an earlier industrial culture, urges them to reject both uncertainty and the condition of dependence inherent in the CIG.

Concern for professional and for social identity can have contrary effects on strategies adopted by the *cassa-integrati*. On the one hand, self-satisfaction and the image of a past role can drive workers to act against their interests; some trade union militants tend to remain in the CIG to the bitter end so as to maintain a link with the firms where they counted for something, whereas for others, the network of contacts built up thanks to their union experience enables them to exit swiftly and advantageously from the CIG. On the other hand, an identity allows those with a role to play to acquire the stability needed in the long term to be able to see ahead and adopt a rational course of action. Many rapid exits, where no prospect of employment exists, can be attributed to the disintegration of a worker's sense of identity in a large firm, which either annihilates his strategic capabilities or forces him even to give up fostering this identity. Family responsibilities ought to keep in check strategies adopted by *cassa-integrati*, but these strategies may diverge according to the employment market. Family men should leave the CIG more quickly than others to re-enter employment, but when unemployment is very low and it is easy to get taken on, they may prolong job-searching and go for work that is better paid. A degree of imprecision as to the family's impact in strictly economic terms in no way diminishes the crucial influence it has on exiting from the CIG. The probability of finding another job is matched against the number of those in the family who already have one; equally the network of social relationships linked with the family as with the inner circle of friends or work colleagues is plainly the means preferred towards finding a new job. At a low level information, if it is hard to come by, depends above all on such closely linked networks (family, friends, close acquaintances). The majority of *cassa-integrati* find their new jobs in small firms or as self-employed, in which cases economic relationships and work relationships are governed by the traditional channels of personal, family and neighbourhood relationships. In the diffuse economy of the small firm and self-employment, just as in the underground economy of unofficial occupations, the labour market is also a 'market for life' in which the worker is selling not just his work strengths but his whole person, together with his family and his social relationships.

Notes

1. Unemployment benefit for the industrial and services sectors in Italy has not been in existence for long, and there are many conditions to be met for it to be available.
2. It needs to be borne in mind that the extent of our knowledge about the *cassa-integrati* is somewhat approximate, based as it is on isolated surveys, and that the only consistent and reliable information concerns non-working hours paid for by the state. By dividing the volume of hours by the average number of hours the figure for *cassa-integrati* is obtained, but the figure does not conform to the real situation since it includes part *cassa-integrati* who continue to work part-time.
3. Statistics from Italian sources used from now on overestimate the unemployment rate in relation to adjusted Eurostat figures, since they include among unemployed even jobless persons who by their own admission are not actively engaged in job-search.
4. Reyneri, 1992. The survey deals with unemployed who have been officially registered for over twelve months and who include those most deprived and excluded as well as those whose motivation in job search is very low because they are following alternative survival strategies, in the submerged economy or within the family.

5. For a résumé on this point see Accornero, 1987.
6. The case of moonlighting has received plenty of study in Italy. For an overview see Gallino, 1985; more generally in connection with the submerged economy, see Bettio and Villa, 1989.

CHAPTER 5

SPAIN: MODERNISATION OF UNEMPLOYMENT

Luis Toharia

Spain is characterised by very high unemployment rates and a considerable number of long-term unemployed. It is also the European country that has undergone the widest variations in employment. In the course of the second half of the 1980s, the Spanish economy registered very marked increases in employment without their leading to commensurate reductions in unemployment. The high decline in employment during the 1990s has aggravated the problem.

General evolution of employment and unemployment

During the 1960s and early 1970s, the Spanish economy registered extremely high economic growth rates, but the rise in employment was the less spectacular because of the pick-up in productivity. Moreover, the industrial fabric created during this period responded less to the needs of international competition than to the efforts of the Franco dictatorship to go for growth at all costs and to develop an area of heavy industry, considered vital for the national economy. The policy resulted in a lop-sided pattern of industrialisation, which was isolated in relation to the international economy and protected from foreign competition.

The economic recession set off by the oil crisis in 1973 had a delayed impact in Spain, because the final governments of the Franco regime, taken up with the growing demands of workers, were unable to make appropriate adjustments when required. Consequently, when political change got underway in 1976 the economy was marked by a latent recession whose effects were not felt internally thanks to an accommodation monetary policy.

From 1977 onwards, political normalisation and the start of the process of opening up the Spanish economy were accompanied by a marked decrease in employment which lasted until 1985. Although data are incomplete, it would appear that these job losses followed on the shutting down of small and medium-sized firms. Forty years of unchallenged rule by employers had left them unable to meet market demand or solve their problems of internal organisation for want of an acceptable policy in the matter of human resources.

From 1980 onwards, and with promulgation of the Workers Charter (Ley del Estatuto de los Trabajadores, referred to subsequently as LET), the prospects of redundancy increased. LET established a precise and fairly exhaustive list of the prospects of redundancy for economic reasons, as well as of the relatively moderate compensation, together with clearly specified ways of calculating the amount. The powers of decision of the judges charged with ruling on cases of redundancy were in practice severely limited by mechanisms for arbitration, mediation and conciliation set up by LET, as well as by the methods of calculating redundancy payment. Consequently, during the second phase of the recession job losses were more closely linked to the adjustment of a firm's workforce than to closures.

The 1982 elections and the political upheaval that followed, with tremendous popular support for the Socialist Party, made no difference to the evolution of employment, which continued to fall in a manner apparently unrelated to political events. However, the end result of the whole period between 1976 and 1986 was an overall loss of jobs representing an estimated 1.9 million wage-earners in the private sector. The losses of jobs in the non-wage earning agricultural sectors (small independent farmers and family workers) were made up for by the marked growth of the public sector and by resorting to independent non-agricultural labour to recoup the losses in wage-earning employment.

The situation righted itself from the middle of 1985 onwards when the Spanish economy started to create employment at a rate unknown even in the peak years of the 1960s growth. Between 1985 and 1991, 1.7 million jobs were created. The number corresponds to the wage-earning jobs in the private sector, growth in the public sector having continued to compensate for the losses of non-wage earning jobs (agricultural and other). Job creation was particularly high until mid-1990, losing impetus in 1991, with the crisis in the Persian Gulf and the restrictive measures adopted by the government in an attempt to curb inflation deemed to be excessive in the context of EMS, which the peseta had joined in 1989.

Although the causes of this marked recovery in employment are much debated, it would appear to be the result of a combination of forces favourable to economic growth, and to the growth of employment in particular. The world economic recovery that began in 1983, helped by the falls in oil prices, was followed by Spain's entry into the European Community in 1986. Measures designed to make the labour market more flexible were subsequently adopted in 1984 to provide the best conditions for the fixed-term contracts that officially came into existence in 1977, but whose application was limited by LET (although a decree issued in 1982 had already relaxed some of the existing constraints).

The world economic recession of the early 1990s has had a strong impact on unemployment, only partially cushioned by the staging of major international events such as the Olympic Games in Barcelona and Expo'92 held in Seville. However, 1993 was the worst in Spain's recent history for employment and growth is only expected to begin again by 1995.

All in all, during the last twenty years, the Spanish economy and the evolution of employment have followed a course leading them back to the point from which they started, though without a comparable pattern in unemployment. In the Franco period, the continuous growth of employment coupled with the pronounced emigration of Spaniards chiefly to the more highly-developed European economies (notably Germany, Switzerland and France) and the low rates of female participation enabled the Spanish economy to avoid the problem of unemployment. The unemployment rate was very low, in the order of 1 to 2 per cent of the working population, but as with all under-developed economies, under-employment was probably a significant factor. During this period the working population and employment were able to grow in parallel at a fairly moderate but constantly positive rate.

The recession brought unemployment in its wake. Between 1976 and 1981 the working population remained virtually constant while employment began to fall. The second phase in the recession saw the working population resuming its rate of growth with employment moderating its fall. The generations of the Spanish 'baby boom' from the second half of the 1960s were coming into the labour market, the boom itself the result of a rise in the birth rate, which was never in fact very high, and more particularly of a marked drop in infant mortality. The result was that in 1985 unemployment passed the 3 million mark, 21 per cent of the working population. Furthermore, the overall rate of activity was down: had it stayed at its 1974 level, the figure would have been 4.5 million, over 30 per cent.

The recent upturn in the economy has improved the position, but only a little. Employment rose by 1.7 million between 1985 and 1991, unemployment dropped by only 600,000, on account of the increase in the working population as soon as conditions for employment turned more favourable. Did those who were unemployed in 1985 take advantage of the upturn in employment, or were they supplanted by those who had newly arrived in the labour market? In other words, did the unemployed of 1985, very many of whom had been unemployed for a long time, simply remain trapped in their condition of long-term unemployed? The data by gender suggest a more positive answer: if in 1985 the proportion of women in overall unemployment was around 30 per cent, in 1991 it was well over the 50 per cent mark, in spite of a significant increase in female employment, which represented nearly half the total number of jobs created.

The long-term unemployed

The course taken by unemployment portrayed here explains why the number of long-term unemployed increased significantly. Indeed, in 1976, with an overall unemployment rate of 5 per cent, long-term unemployed counted for 18 per cent. In 1986 the respective figures reached 21 per cent and 57 per cent. In 1987 long-term unemployed stood at 63 per cent, but the figure is not comparable with the preceding ones and since then it has clearly come down to its present level (second quarter 1991) of 51 per cent. This last figure is still very high, but so too is the overall rate of unemployment.

The evolution of these two components of unemployment has varied by gender. The number of male unemployed, taken with the percentage of long-term unemployed, has undergone quite an appreciable decline in the course of recent years. With women the course taken was different depending on whether they had or had not worked already. Female unemployed seeking their first job decreased in number, but the percentage of those in search of a job for over a year has remained at extremely high levels (in the order of 80 per cent). On the other hand, female unemployed with a job behind them have grown in number, but in their case the percentage of long-term unemployed shows a clear drop. The explanation for these contrasting patterns evidently lies in the differing pace of the net outflows from unemployment (i.e. inflows minus outflows). In the case of male unemployed, these flows have been very strong, but in the case of women the situation has been varied. For female unemployed in first job search for a year or more, net outflows have been positive but not pronounced enough to reduce their impact on overall unemployment. In the case of female unemployed who have had jobs, increase in overall figures suggests an inflow of new entrants to unemployment (short-term in the first instance). This would explain the reductions in percentage of the long-term unemployed in spite of the increase in their absolute number. The problem of long-term unemployment does not appear to contain a female component more pronounced than does overall unemployment, clearly weighted on the side of women.

When the figures are broken down for each of the 17 Spanish regions (autonomous communities), it is observed that the 3 regions which display the highest unemployment rates (Andalusia, Estremadura and the Canaries) show a relatively reduced long-term unemployment figure, close to the average for Spain, and that the 3 northern regions (Asturias, Cantabria and the Basque country) show an unemployment rate in the neighbourhood of the average for Spain, but much higher percentages in the case of long-term unemployment. In the first case, this is due partly to the special aid programmes for agricultural employment (which do not in fact apply to the Canaries), and also to the highly seasonal character of the regions' basic activities (agriculture, tourism and construction trades). In these three regions long-term unemployment does not present a specific problem; it is open to many to find jobs, albeit temporary ones, after which they return to unemployment. Certainly, insofar as the process of exiting from and re-entering unemployment is a recurrent one, it is possible to talk of long-term unemployment, since the overall unemployment rate is high. But there is no one group of unemployed whose prospects are nil. The regions in the north have seen major industrial restructuring (in particular, the Asturias and the Basque country), and with it special measures to safeguard employment. But in these regions long-term unemployment does constitute a specific problem.

The system of unemployment insurance in Spain, as in most European countries, is one where payment of benefit is conditional on a minimum working period. Legislation lays it down that the span for benefit shall be equal to half that of contributions, with a minimum of six months contributions and a maximum of twenty-four months benefit. Voluntarily leaving a job affords the one exception to the right of receiving benefit. For example a person who works for six months on a fixed-term contract, when its term has run, is entitled to three months unemployment benefit. The legal benefit rate is 80 per cent of the wage for the first 6 months unemployment, then 70 per cent for the following 6 months and 60 per cent for the final 12 months. The minimum amount is the legal minimum wage (equivalent in 1991 to about £325), in the order of 40 per cent of the average wage, and the maximum between 170 per cent and 220 per cent of guaranteed minimum wage, depending on family commitments. After 24 months a person unemployed is entitled to so-called assistance benefit if he/she has a dependent family or is over 45, the benefit varying between 75 per cent and 125 per cent of the legal minimum wage. Furthermore, the maximum period for which unemployed persons are entitled to receive support benefit is 18 months unless they are over 45, in which case it may be extended to 30 months and even indefinitely for those over 52. INEM (Ministry of Employment; see Appendix) figures give about 50 per cent receiving unemployment benefit and 50 per cent support benefit among those who are unemployed and in receipt of benefit. Moreover, in the majority of cases support benefit concerns people who are relatively old, men in the main. Figures are not available for the actual level of allowances in relation to previous earnings. In addition, 38 per cent of unemployed state they are registered and in receipt of benefit, 45 per cent male and 30 per cent female, 42 per cent of those unemployed having been so for under two years and 28 per cent for two years or more.

Furthermore, according to LFS (the Labour Force Survey; see Appendix) in the second quarter of 1991 more than 60,000 employed workers and nearly 200,000 jobless claim to have received unemployment benefit, among them older men no longer in job search since they count on receiving unemployment benefit until retirement and married women whose husbands are employed and who have dependent children. The same source shows that the number of households receiving no unemployment benefit is very limited. Hence welfare cover for the unemployed, however long they have been so, is almost complete, which is not to say of course that the amount paid is necessarily adequate.

What are the factors accounting for long-term unemployment being so high in Spain? In the case of men, the parallel course of unemployment and long-term unemployment makes it clear that as problems they are not unrelated; this much is suggested by the marked parallel drop in the figures for both over recent years. For women the situation is quite different, and this is shown in the discrepancy between women who are looking for a first job and those with work experience behind them.

Married women (more especially those with young children), older women, those who are less qualified (in terms of schooling and subsequent training), those whose commitment to job seeking is less evident, those in receipt of unemployment benefit, those who have been longer unemployed and, finally, those without access to appropriate channels seem the most under threat of long-term unemployment.

Econometric analysis based on the LFS survey referred to draws a comparison between long-term unemployed and those who have shown themselves capable of making an exit by finding a job:

- First, the probabilities of finding a job are much lower for women. This might appear paradoxical given the high increase in female employment, in the order of half the employment created during the upturn of recent years. This is not the case, however, since entry into employment from being without a job has been higher for women than for men, which implies that unemployed women have been exceeded by those who are non-working.
- Second, age is a decisive factor. In the case of women, age has a constant, negative influence on the probability of finding a job that allows an exit from unemployment. With men, a falling-off occurs only after 30 but then it is more pronounced.
- In regard to education, the skills indicator applied does not seem to exert an influence where men are concerned but in the case of women a university degree is a powerful asset to the chances of leaving unemployment.
- Family situation exerts a fundamental influence. Being spouse (male or female) of the head of the household reduces the probability of exiting from unemployment very considerably, thus increasing that of long-term unemployment. Evidently, the case applies above all to women, men who are spouses of the head of the household representing only a trifling percentage of the unemployed.
- Facility of access to suitable channels for finding a job is also an advantage in leaving unemployment, notably in households where another person is in employment, while there being someone unemployed in the family lowers the chances of finding employment.
- Findings have not made it possible to throw light directly on the extent to which unemployment benefit, purposeful job search and length of unemployment play a part. Analysis elsewhere, however, suggests that being a married woman inevitably inhibits the intensity of looking for a job.
- Length of time spent unemployed seems to exert a negative effect on the probability of leaving unemployment, with men in particular. Nearly a third of short-term unemployed (i.e. under twelve months) find themselves becoming long-term unemployed, and the probability of becoming so permanently exceeds 50 per cent when the spell has lasted over a year. With women the figures are 50 per cent and 60 per cent respectively. The probabilities of persistence have shown a pronounced drop in recent years; in 1987–8 the figures for men were roughly 40 per cent and 60 per cent and for women 70 per cent and 75 per cent.

How to fight long-term unemployment in Spain?

The evidence in this chapter makes it clear that long-term unemployment is not a structural problem independent of the overall problem of unemployment, since the proportion of long-term unemployment has followed a course parallel to the overall unemployment rate, increasing during the recession and diminishing with recovery. This is especially true where men are concerned. With women the situation is more complex. But unemployment has taken on a feminine character. Women now represent more than half the total of unemployed, compared with a third in 1985. The unemployment rate for women is twice that for men and the proportion of long-term unemployment in female unemployment is appreciably higher than is the case with men.

Long-term unemployment in Spain does not seem to be a function of level of attainment as measured by schooling. As it happens new employment in Spain over the last six years has not called for a high level of schooling. The protection afforded in Spain for the unemployed would seem to be generous enough, not that benefits are high, but because virtually all the unemployed benefit from them, either directly or via other members of the family.

In the fight against unemployment, in particular long-term unemployment, a first response is still the provision of training, and second the reduction of unemployment benefit, generally thought to be a disincentive to job seeking. In the Spanish context neither notion seems appropriate. In an economy that has managed to create two million jobs in the last six years, it is hard to believe that raising the level of education or training would lead to further overall reduction in unemployment, particularly long-term. Naturally, in individual cases – and with women more than men – higher educational attainment would seem to make it easier to exit from unemployment, but it is an argument that does not have general application nor provide ground for adoption as a policy. Although existing data do not permit analyses that are totally satisfying, it would seem that the impact of unemployment benefit on the degree of activeness in job searching is not very considerable, especially where long-term unemployment is concerned. A policy of reducing such benefits would pose problems for the unemployed, without making their exit from unemployment more likely. In the medium- and long-term the creation of a growing number of stable jobs seems the only viable solution. Problems of unemployment in Spain in our opinion continue to be problems of lack of jobs, and not problems of labour supply linked to attitudes on the part of the unemployed deemed to be inefficient.

Appendix

Long-term unemployment: problems of statistical definition

In Spain, as in other European countries, there exist two sources of data on unemployment: the data of the labour force survey (Encuesta de Poblacion Activa, elsewhere referred to here as LFS) and the number of persons registered as unemployed under INEM (Institute Nacional de Emples), government job centres. Data in the first case are from a nationwide sample of 60,000 families established in accordance with rigorous statistical criteria. In order to be declared unemployed, a respondent has to satisfy three criteria: not to have worked even for one hour during the preceding week; to have searched for a job over the preceding four weeks; and to be in a position to accept a possible offer of employment within a fortnight.

Data in the second case come from an administrative census of people who make a voluntary statement to the effect that they are without a job and that they would like one. Consequently they reflect peoples' intentions, intentions which, in turn, reflect their perception of the possibilities on offer from the job centres as well as those of finding an acceptable job, and, in addition, of having access to public welfare benefits, such as unemployment benefit, priority in recruitment according to length of time registered as unemployed, subsidised occupational training schemes, etc. These characteristics dictate that the figures submitted by INEM do not have statistical value: the rate of unemployment measured by the percentage of unemployed registered under INEM in relation to the labour force (LFS's figures) is simply erroneous.

A comparison of figures taken from both sources shows that some persons who, according to LFS, are employed or jobless are nonetheless registered under INEM (926,000 for the second quarter 1991, 255,000 of whom declare they are receiving unemployment benefit). There are also unemployed who are not registered under INEM, though their number, 195,000, is lower.

So far as length of unemployment is concerned, INEM data would make it possible to monitor individuals on entry and on exit in INEM files. Unfortunately this source is not exploited in Spain. The LFS requires people who state they are seeking work (some of whom clearly are unemployed) to declare how long this has been the case, which is a measure of the 'length of time spent in unemployment' (rather than the 'duration' of unemployment) at a given moment. Even so, it is impossible to monitor the whole experience of a spell of unemployment from entry into exit. So it is that the term 'long-term unemployed' is applied to those who state they have been unemployed for at least a year, whereas a more appropriate term would be 'long-standing unemployed'. It is important to be clear about the meaning of terms.

A change in method was introduced into the LFS in 1987 in order to come into line with European Community norms. Until then the questions put were closed: the interviewer offered the respondent a choice between various clearly drafted possibilities. Now the questions are open-ended, with the respondent being asked the number of months or years (if the months exceed 23) spent in job search. The effect of this apparently anodyne change has been to increase the percentage of long-term unemployed, in a way that may suggest itself as artificial, without making too much of it. It has also led to some improvements. For instance, since 1987, LFS asks people what their situation was a year prior to the survey, which allows a comparison to be made between those who state they were in employment at the time of the survey but unemployed a year previously, and those who state they were unemployed at the time of the survey and a year previously. In other words, it is now possible to compare those who exit from unemployment into a job with those unemployed who remain unemployed.

From the point of view of the problem of unemployment becoming permanent, the comparison touched upon above is one of the two fundamental questions: namely, are there particular features preventing unemployed people from finding a way out of their situation so that they become long-term unemployed? The other important question has to do with inflows into unemployment: are there particular features which favour entry into unemployment? Unfortunately, it is not easy to find an answer to the second question with the LFS data such as they exist at the present time. To be in a position to do so would require setting up longitudinal data with the aim of monitoring individuals over a period of time. In principle this is possible and to a certain extent in conjunction with EPA, but here is probably one of the important and as yet unfinished tasks of the Spanish Statistical Office.

CHAPTER 6

SOCIAL CONSEQUENCES OF LONG-TERM UNEMPLOYMENT IN BRITAIN

Duncan Gallie

The material and social deprivation caused by unemployment in the great depression of the 1930s was movingly documented in a range of different studies (Jahoda *et al*, 1972; Bakke, 1933; the Pilgrim Trust Report, 1938). It was clear that loss of work brought about poverty, severe psychological distress and the collapse of sociability. The most famous study of this period – that of Marienthal – showed how unemployment led eventually to the complete disintegration of community life.

One of the central objectives underlying the construction of the welfare state in Britain in the post-war period was to ensure that unemployment would never again be the scourge to human welfare that it had proved to be in the inter-war period. This was to be achieved partly through the pursuit of macroeconomic policies that were designed to keep unemployment to a very low level. But it was also to be realized by the provision of a system of financial support for the unemployed, which would protect those without work from poverty and the psychological deterioration that accompanied it. An important and distinctive characteristic of the system of financial assistance to the unemployed that was introduced in Britain was that it guaranteed a stable source of income for the entire period for which a person was unemployed.

When mass unemployment returned in the 1980s, the effectiveness of this system of support was to be put to its crucial test. Was it the case that the creation of the welfare state had fundamentally altered the experience of unemployment and that it was no longer the social curse that it had been in an earlier era? This issue was to be a major preoccupation of British social research in the 1980s. This chapter will examine some of the conclusions that can be drawn about the effects of unemployment on people's experience of financial deprivation, on their psychological well-being, on their families, on their social networks and on their wider social and political attitudes.

The financial implications of unemployment

There can be little doubt that the British welfare system in the 1980s provided a much more effective shield against extremes of poverty than the mixture of insurance systems and charity support that prevailed in the 1930s. From this point of view the British unemployed were also considerably better placed in terms of the lenght of time over which they could rely on financial assistance than, for instance, their French equivalents (see Chapter 2). However, the research evidence points clearly to the fact that unemployment in the 1980s still involved heavy financial deprivation and that financial anxieties remained a major source of strain in the everyday lives of the unemployed.

The most comprehensive study of the material implications of unemployment was the national survey, *Living Standards during Unemployment*, carried out in 1983–4 (Heady and Smyth, 1989). This was a longitudinal study that followed 2925 unemployed main family earners over a period of 15 months. A first point to note is the very sharp fall in family income that followed unemployment. The study reports that, after 3 months unemployment, the average disposable income of families whose head had previously been in full-time work was 59 per cent of what it had been before signing on. Most families experienced a rapid and substantial reduction in their material living standards, with particularly sharp reductions in food, clothing and entertainments. It is clear, then, that the view that welfare benefits provided a level of support that eradicated the financial benefits of employment has little empirical support. However, a second important conclusion of the study was that nearly all the reduction in these areas of consumption appears to have taken place in the first three months of unemployment. There was a slight further reduction in average levels of consumption between the third and fifteenth month of signing on – but only in the case of older informants and their families (Heady and Smyth, 1989: xvii). The severe financial effects of unemployment take place relatively early on and, in this respect, the long-term unemployed do not form a distinctive group.

The broad picture provided by income data is confirmed by the accounts given by the unemployed of their experience of deprivation. A rich source of information on the experiences of the unemployed is the data from the Social Change and Economic Life Initiative (henceforth

SCELI). This included interviews in 1986–7 with 871 unemployed, 4047 employed and 1156 non-active people in six British localities – Aberdeen, Coventry, Kirkcaldy, Northampton, Rochdale and Swindon. It is notable that, when asked what were the main disadvantages of being unemployed, by far the most frequent type of response was financial. Overall, 66 per cent of unemployed people reported this as the single most important disadvantage they experienced. Further, the unemployed were very much more likely to be experiencing financial difficulty. Whereas some 70 per cent of the unemployed found their current financial situation either very or quite difficult, this was the case for only 23 per cent of people in employment.

There was little evidence, however, that the experience of financial deprivation grew very much sharper among the long-term unemployed. The proportion finding their current financial situation very or quite difficult rose from 62 per cent among those unemployed for less than 6 months, to 72 per cent among those unemployed for 6 to 12 months to 78 per cent among those unemployed for more than 12 months. In general, the major difference lies between the unemployed as a whole and those in employment rather than between different groups of the uemployed.

Were unemployed women more protected from financial deprivation than unemployed men? The overall pattern is very similar for men and women; unemployment brings a sharp increase in financial deprivation for both. But men report a higher level of deprivation and this is particularly marked with longer spells of unemployment. More detailed analysis shows that this can be almost entirely attributed to the availability of income from a partner. Unemployed women are more likely than unemployed men to have a partner that is employed and this helps to maintain a higher level of household income. This does not necessarily mean, however, that the effects of unemployment on women's personal expenditure are less than they are for men. There is some evidence that men and women cope with the financial costs of unemployment in somewhat different ways. Perhaps because of their household responsibilities, women were particularly likely to make economies when they became unemployed by cutting back on food and expenditure on clothing, whereas men were more likely to go into debt.

Psychological consequences

The inter-war studies of unemployment highlighted the acute psychological demoralisation that accompanied unemployment. It was shown to have led over time to personal withdrawal and to a collapse of interest even in relatively costless leisure activities. It could be argued that this reflected a period in which unemployment posed much more acute problems of financial survival. However, Jahoda (1982) has suggested that the importance of employment for psychological stability lies less in the money that it brings than in the fact that it fulfils a number of vital latent functions. It provides an enforced pattern of activity, it gives people a clear time structure to the day, it is a source of social contacts outside the household, it gives people a sense of participating in a wider collective purpose, and it is a source of social status and identity. If this view is correct, a decline in financial hardship would not eliminate the root causes of psychological distress.

In the 1980s a major programme of research into the psychological consequences of unemployment was launched in Britain by the Social and Applied Psychology Unit at Sheffield, under the direction of Peter Warr. These studies showed that unemployment led consistently to higher levels of psychological distress among men. The effects of unemployment were shown to be as strong for middle-class as for working-class men (Payne *et al.,* 1984). They were significant among all age groups, although they were particularly strong among middle-aged men (Warr and Jackson, 1984). Since many of these studies were cross-sectional it might be objected that it was difficult to disentangle cause and effect. However, a longitudinal study (Warr and Jackson, 1985) showed that once people returned to employment, there was a marked improvement in their psychological well-being, indicating that unemployment was the real causal factor.

There is rather less evidence available about the effect of different durations of unemployment on psychological distress. However, Warr and Jackson compared the reports of changes in psychological health for people unemployed for different lengths of time. This showed that the psychological health of men unemployed for more than three months was significantly worse than that of men out of work for shorter periods. However, the decline in psychological health then levelled out and there was no evidence of further deterioration after about 3 months. The researchers conclude that:

The initial movement into the unemployed role is likely to be followed by an increased number of threatening events, as a person strives to deal with official benefit agencies, learns about job-seeking procedures, adopts new patterns of interaction with family members, and assesses him or herself in relation to personal values and societal pressures. This initial period is likely to be one of considerable turbulance and threat, the levels of which gradually decline as an unemployed person finds that previously new situations have become familiar and the frequency of novel threatening events has declined. In addition a person is likely gradually to adapt him or herself to the unemployed role. Daily and weekly routines become established, expenditure limits become clarified, and behaviour may be shaped to avoid threats from new situations or other people (Warr and Jackson, 1985: 805).

The main factors that made a difference to psychological health over the period were the age of the unemployed person (with middle-aged men with family responsibilities particularly vulnerable), the initial level of people's commitment to employment and the extent to which they could rely on someone to offer financial help when they were in need. An interesting feature of their data was that financial stress was unrelated to change in psychological well-being over the month, giving some support to the Jahoda thesis.

The Warr and Jackson sample was restricted in two important respects: it was confined to the non-skilled manual, working-class and to men. The national survey on Living Standards during Unemployment also included a measure of psychological well-being, that made it possible to compare a representative sample of all unemployed men after three months and fifteen months of unemployment. The authors report that: 'The Overall picture is static – there were no significant falls or rises in the average psychological well-being scores of either the sampled informants or their wives.' (Heady and Smyth, 1989: 63). There is no national evidence yet available that covers both unemployed men and unemployed women, but the SCELI data enable us to examine the problem for a cross-section of the population of six local labour markets. As can be seen in Table 6.1 the overall scores for psychological distress for people with different durations of unemployment are very close indeed and the major divide is between the unemployed and those in employment. More detailed analysis of the data shows that

Table 6.1
Psychological distress
(Scores in GHQ test*)

	Overall	Men	Women
Self-employed	3,11	3,16	3,05
Wage-earners	3,15	3,03	3,32
Unemployed < 6 mths	4,66	4,59	4,80
Unemployed 6–12 mths	4,69	4,67	5,13
Unemployed 12 mths +	4,64	4,68	4,50
Non-working	3,75	4,15	3,71

*The higher the indicator, the greater the psychological distress.

there is no statistically significant difference in psychological distress between people with different durations of unemployment and, similarly, there is no significant difference between men and women.

Unemployment and family life

Unemployment and family tension

There were clear indications in the inter-war literature that the psychological consequences of unemployment spilled over from the individual directly affected to the family as a whole. In more recent research, this has been confirmed by a number of small-scale qualitative studies. For instance, McKee and Bell (1985, 1986) found that male unemployment sharply increased family divisiveness. A major source of conflict was the management of scarce financial resources, with sharp disagreements about what money was to be spent on and whom it was to be spent on. But a number of other factors also contributed to greater tension in the family. The presence of the father at home every day led to conflict about who had authority over the children. Wives found they were confronted with an increase in the amount of housework they had to cope with, while the conditions for carrying it out were less easy. A similar picture of sharply increased strain in the family emerged from the work of Fagin and Little (1984). They point to the way in which tension could develop between partners over the responsibility for failing to find work.

Many wives after months of job search, with relationships under severe strain, and continual worries about making ends meet, began to reproach their partners, implicitly or explicitly, for their circumstances. This external confirmation of inadequacy by a close member of the family had a dramatic impact on the morale of the men, who then felt further misunderstood and resorted to isolation within the family (Fagin and Little, 1984: 51).

There has been much less survey-based research on family tension than on individual psychological consequences. However, the 1983–4 national survey of *Living Standards during Unemployment* investigated the psychological well-being not only of the unemployed men that formed the central focus of the study, but also of their wives. Their results showed clearly that the distress of unemployment affected partners as well. Indeed:

In all the family-type and age categories the husbands tended to record slightly higher levels of psychological welfare than their wives despite the husband being the person that had directly experienced the trauma of losing his job. This difference cannot be explained in terms of the level of financial anxiety, since husbands reported on average a slightly greater amount of time spent worrying about money than did their wives (Heady and Smyth, 1989: 63,66).

Overall, the authors conclude that the husband's unemployment had almost as much impact on the psychological well-being of his wife as it did on his own feelings of well-being.

Evidence from the SCELI research programme in the mid-1980s also showed that unemployment had a major impact on the perceived quality of family life. Over 90 per cent of both unemployed men and unemployed women felt that unemployment caused tension in the family and over 65 per cent were strongly of this view. Indeed, family tension emerged as the consequence of unemployment that was felt most sharply after individual anxiety; it was notably more important than either poverty or loss of respect.

Unemployment also affected the extent to which people were satisfied with their family lives. The evidence here suggests a difference in the experiences of unemployed men and unemployed women. Satisfaction with family life was markedly lower among unemployed men than among those that were employed, even where unemployment had lasted for less than six months. Moreover, the longer the time that men had been unemployed, the greater their dissatisfaction. Among women, in contrast, those unemployed for less than six months showed higher levels of satisfaction with family life than women in employment and satisfaction was even greater among those unemployed for six to twelve months. It is only among women unemployed for more than twelve months that satisfaction declines. It seems likely that this pattern reflects the fact that unemployment initially resolves some of the tensions for women of trying to reconcile heavy domestic responsibilities with the demands of a job. They are able to devote more time to their partner, children and other home activities, without feeling, to the same degree as men, the pressure to return to employment. In general, the qualitative evidence suggests that unemployment is highly threatening to the male identity in the family, while it seems unlikely that this is the case to the same degree for women.

While a number of studies now provide converging evidence of the implications of unemployment for friction in the family, there is much less evidence about whether this friction is sufficiently intense to increase the probability that a person's marriage will collapse. However, Lampard (1990) has examined the detailed chronology of spells of unemployment and marital dissolution, while controlling for a wide range of background factors that might also affect the chances of marital break-up. His evidence points firmly to the conclusion that unemployment does directly increase the risk of marital dissolution. The marriage of an unemployed person was 2.3 times as likely to end in the following year as the marriage of a person that had never been unemployed.

Unemployment and family work careers

Apart from its costs in terms of increased tension in the family, there is considerable evidence that male unemployment has serious implications for the work careers of other family members. To begin with, in Britain, as in several other countries, there is a clear tendency for the wives of unemployed men to be markedly less likely to be in employment than the wives of employed men. For instance, the second DHSS Cohort study, carried out in 1987, reported that 40 per cent of the female partners of the male unemployed were in employment, compared with 60 per cent of married women of working age (Ehrens and Hedges, 1990: 72–73).

There has been extensive debate about how such differences are to be explained, ranging from views that emphasise the shared character of local labour market conditions, through arguments about the sub-cultural characteristics of unemployed families to theories in terms of the disincentive effects of the welfare benefits system. The 1978 DHSS Cohort study showed that the rate of employment of the wives of men in their sample was already very low before the men registered as unemployed, although the lack of systematic work history data made it impossible to assess whether this could be accounted for in terms of earlier experiences of unemployment. There was, however, a clear decline in the proportion of wives in employment as the duration of employment increased. Exactly the same pattern emerges from the 1980 MSC Cohort study where the proportion of wives in employment fell from 33 per cent to 25 per cent between the first and tenth month of unemployment (Daniel, 1990: 182, 191).

Moreover, there was a strong indication that the nature of the benefit system was an important factor leading women to give up their jobs. The British system provides two types of income support for the unemployed: unemployment benefit and supplementary benefit. It is primarily supplementary benefit, which was designed to provide a safety net for the longer-term unemployed, that is likely to act as a disincentive to the wife continuing in employment. Unless she earned more than her husband's benefit, the system of earnings deductions meant that she received little financial advantage from earning. When the unemployed were compared in terms of the type of benefit they were receiving, it was clear that wives were much more likely to leave employment when their husbands were on supplementary benefit than when they were on unemployment benefit (Moylan *et al.*, 128–130). Further confirmation of the pattern comes from the 1980 MSC Cohort study, which found that the decline in wives' employment was particularly marked among women in part-time work, whose low earnings would make them particularly vulnerable to the disincentive effect of the supplementary benefit procedures. In short, the design of the welfare system would appear to reinforce the tendency for unemployment to be concentrated in households and for the unemployed to become increasingly isolated from contact with the labour market as the duration of unemployment increases.

Moreover, there is evidence to suggest that the effect of unemployment may not only affect the partners' work career, but also that of the children. In an analysis of General Household Survey data for 1980–1981, Payne (1987:208) has shown that whether or not the head of household was unemployed had important implications for young people's unemployment. Where the head of household was unemployed the odds of unemployment for young people were doubled and this disadvantage grew even sharper if the head of household had been unemployed for more than a year. Unlike the situation for the wives of unemployed men, this intergenerational concentration of unemployment could not be attributed to the welfare benefits system. A young person that was no longer at school would be treated as independent and their earnings would not be deducted from the head of household's benefit. It seems rather that parental unemployment produces a level of demoralisation and a degree of isolation from contacts with the labour market that severely undermines the career opportunities of children.

Unemployment and sociability

In contrast to the picture provided by the inter-war literature of virtually complete social withdrawal by the unemployed, research in the 1980s has indicated that the unemployed continue to keep an active leisure life and to participate in social networks that extend beyond the immediate household (Miles, 1983; Trew and Kilpatrick, 1983). At the same time, however, there is evidence that unemployment has significant consequences for the nature of both leisure and sociability.

In the SCELI local labour market research, leisure participation rates were calculated on the basis of a wide range of different leisure activities, using both questionnaire and time budget methods. The overall levels of leisure activity of the unemployed and the employed were virtually identical. However, there was evidence of a qualitative shift in the types of leisure engaged in, with the unemployed turning to less expensive forms of leisure activity. The fact that the level of involvement in leisure activities remained very similar between the employed and the unemployed was quite compatible, of course, with the fact that the unemployed also experienced much longer periods of dead time during the day and, indeed, boredom was the most commonly cited disadvantage of unemployment after that of financial difficulty.

Moreover, the unemployed were less likely than the employed to engage in leisure activities with people outside their own households. The extent to which this occured depended on the particular characteristics of the unemployed person. Lower sociability was most marked among single people, whereas married women were affected much less. The pattern by length of unemployment is particularly interesting. In the first year of unemployment, there was a marked tendency for sociability to decline. For both men and women, sociability was substantially lower among those unemployed between six months and a year than among those unemployed for six months or less. However, the trend then reverses and there is an increase in sociability among the long-term unemployed. Among men, sociability still remains lower than in the early months of unemployment, but among women the long-term unemployed show the highest level of sociability of any group of the unemployed. This suggests that there may be some process of adaptation to unemployment among the long-term unemployed. This may be facilitated for women by their distinctive patterns of sociability (which rely more heavily on neighbourly visiting) and by a lower stigma attached to women being without work.

As well as the tendency for the frequency of sociability to be lower among the unemployed, there is also a marked difference in the nature of the social networks in which they participate. There appears to be a very high level of segregation between the social networks of the employed and the unemployed. Whereas the networks of the majority of those in employment consisted primarily of other people in work, this was the case for only a minority of the unemployed. Here the effect of duration of unemployment is very marked. For those unemployed for six months or less, 50 per cent still have social networks that consist predominantly of the employed (i.e three-quarters or more of their friends are in employment). However, the proportion falls steeply to 33 per cent among people unemployed for six months to a year and to 31 per cent among the long-term unemployed. These figures conceal, however, an important difference by gender. It is above all among unemployed men that there is a marked change in the composition of networks – with the proportion participating in predominantly employed networks falling from 55 per cent among those unemployed for six months or less to a mere 19 per cent among the long-term unemployed. Among unemployed women, on the other hand, there is very little change at all; even among the long-term unemployed 44 per cent are in networks that are predominately of employed people. Women are also more likely to have friends that are housewives. Hence whereas 49 per cent of long-term unemployed men are in networks where three-quarters or more of their friends are also unemployed, this is the case for only 26 per cent of long-term unemployed women (see Table 6.2).

The nature of people's networks was in turn related to important differences in the extent to which they had access to support in times of difficulty. The unemployed were less likely than the employed to have somebody that they could rely upon if they felt depressed, if they needed financial assistance or if they wanted help in finding a job. This was clearly related to the composition of the networks. The higher the proportion of unemployed people in a person's network, the less likely they were to be able to count on either material or psychological assistance. Access to support also declined sharply with longer durations of unemployment. Whereas 69 per cent of people unemployed for six months or less had strong support networks, this fell to only 47 per cent among the long-term unemployed. This absence of support is particularly striking for unemployed men. Whereas 57 per cent of women that had experienced long-term unemployment still had strong support networks, this was the case for only 38 per cent of long-term unemployed men.

In short, while there may have been some process of adaptation to long-term unemployment in that the decline in sociability was arrested and people may have started to become more involved again in

Table 6.2
Social networks
(as % of those who say that their
friends and mates are all or almost all in employment)

	Men	Women
Self-employed	86	60
Wage-earners	85	78
Unemployed < 6 months	55	45
Unemployed 6–12 months	33	31
Unemployed 12 months +	19	44
Non-working	42	46

external social networks, the nature of these networks had changed quite fundamentally in the case of the male unemployed. They moved from networks that were primarily of people in employment into networks that increasingly consisted of other unemployed people. In the process, they found themselves increasingly cut off from an effective support system that could help them meet financial difficulties, that could give psychological support and that could provide the information about jobs that was needed if people were to escape from the condition of unemployment. Changes in the pattern of sociability, then, increasingly helped to reinforce their exclusion from the labour market.

The political attitudes of the unemployed

For the researchers of the inter-war period, the breakdown of sociability was directly related to the disintegration of forms of political activity. The decline of cultural life was paralleled by a loss of interest in politics; while the withdrawal of individuals into social isolation in their everyday personal relationships undercut any possibility of developing effective collective action with the objective of producing radical social change.

Research in Britain (Marshall *et al.*, 1988) has confirmed that unemployment does not generate radical political ideologies. In terms of their attitudes to class inequality and their general political beliefs, the British unemployed are remarkably similar to workers in employment. However, there is some evidence that unemployment radicalises in a more modest way by increasing the importance that people attach to collectivist as against individualist principles of social organisation.

For instance, in their study of British electoral behaviour in the 1980s, Heath and his colleagues (1991:162–170) found that the unemployed were particularly likely to vote for the Labour party. When the unemployed were compared with other low income groups, they were still much more likely to support the Labour party, suggesting that their political position did not simply reflect the radicalizing effect of financial deprivation. Similarly, when patterns of change in voting behaviour were examined over time, the unemployed were very different from employed working-class people. Whereas the latter underwent a substantial defection from the Labour party over the period 1979 to 1989, the allegiance of the unemployed remained just as strong, while there was a significant erosion of support for the Conservative party. Moreover, the often cited relationship between unemployment and lower voting turnout was accounted for almost entirely by the social background characteristics of the unemployed rather than by unemployment *per se*. In short, unemployment did not lead to greater political apathy. Rather, it consolidated allegiance to the Labour party and prevented the drift to the right that characterised other social groups in the 1980s.

This general picture is reinforced by the evidence from the SCELI research, which examined people's views about redistributive state spending and taxation (Gallie and Vogler, 1990). Favourability to redistributive state spending and taxation can be seen as representing a collectivist orientation to society. The unemployed were clearly more collectivist in their social attitudes than any other labour market group and this remained the case when a wide range of other factors had been taken into account that might have affected people's attitudes, for instance previous class position, age and education. Although people's political allegiances and early political socialization were important for their attachment to collectivism, the effect of unemployment was still evident when these had been taken into account. Further, one of the striking conclusions of the analysis was that the effects of unemployment were evident even after people had returned to employment. Employed people who had experienced unemployment during the previous five years were significantly more collectivist than those that had been continuously employed, even when other background characteristics had been controlled for.

The evidence suggests then, that unemployment at least helps to maintain collectivist attitudes. But does its effect on political orientations grow greater with long durations of unemployment? There is no national level evidence available on this issue, but the SCELI locality data suggests that the impact is felt at a relatively early stage in the experience of unemployment and that long-term unemployment does not lead to further radicalization. As can be seen in Table 6.3 there is little difference at all in the level of collectivism of men that have been unemployed for between six and twelve months and those unemployed for more than a year. Among women, it is those unemployed for between six and twelve months that showed the highest level of collectivism. This fits well with the earlier evidence about the implications of length of unemployment for financial deprivation and psychological distress. In both cases, unemployment led to severe deprivation within a few months and the effects then changed little with longer durations of unemployment. The pattern for political attitudes largely paralleled that of the material and psychological deprivations that underlie them.

Table 6.3
Collectivist values

	Overall	Men	Women
Selft-employed	2,09	1,89	2,56
Wage-earners	3,00	3,02	3,04
Unemployed < 6 mths	3,79	4,20	3,43
Unemployed 6–12 mths	3,94	3,91	4,19
Unemployed 12 mths +	3,91	3,96	3,84
Non-working	2,88	3,39	2,90
N	1814	876	935

Note. The indicator of collectivism is based on six questions to do with redistributive state spending and taxation. The higher the values, the more marked the collectivist orientation to society.

Conclusions

The central conclusion of the research that has been carried out in Britain into the social consequences of unemployment is that neither changes in the composition of the unemployed nor in the provision of welfare have removed the very damaging effects of unemployment on people's material resources, their psychological well-being and their family and social lives. Unemployment continues to lead to a major fall in household income and to a sharp reduction in consumption standards. It leads to substantially higher levels of psychological distress, and this affects not only the unemployed person but also their partner. It produces severe tension within families, markedly lower levels of satisfaction with family life and higher rates of marital break-up. Finally, it is associated with lower levels of sociability and with weaker social support systems, reinforcing the exclusion of the unemployed from the labour market. The experience of these deprivations would appear to have a clear effect on political orientations leading to a reinforcement of collectivist values.

The broad pattern of effects of unemployment is the same for men and for women, although there are some significant differences in their experiences. Men and women experience similar levels of financial difficulty in the early months of unemployment, but financial deprivation is substantially greater for men among the medium- and long-term unemployed. Women's unemployment leads to psychological distress and family tension in the same way as men's. The two notable differences between unemployed men and unemployed women relate to their satisfaction with family life and to their patterns of sociability.

Whereas unemployment leads to progressively greater deterioration in satisfaction with family life among men, women unemployed for less than a year have higher levels of satisfaction than their equivalents in employment. Women also appear to be able to maintain more extensive social networks in the face of long-term unemployment, they are less likely to become segregated into networks consisting predominantly of other unemployed people and they retain higher levels of social support.

While the British welfare system had clearly not removed the deprivations of unemployment, its distinctive structure may have affected the experience of unemployment over time. In Britain, many of the deprivations brought by unemployment strike relatively early and the long-term unemployed would not appear to be as distinctive a category as is sometimes suggested. The sharpest reductions in living standards have been carried out by the third month of unemployment and the decline after that is much less marked. Similarly, psychological well-being declines sharply in the first three months, but subsequently stays at much the same level. The effect of unemployment on political attitudes closely parallels those for financial deprivation and psychological distress. This may reflect a system of financial support for the unemployment that provides a relatively low level of income, but maintains it for the duration of unemployment.

However, if the welfare system may well have been successful in preventing the type of complete financial and psychological collapse that so frequently characterised the inter-war period, it failed to stop the progressive social isolation of the unemployed. The most remorseless effect of long-term unemployment lies in its effects on the social networks of the unemployed. In the first place, long-term male unemployment leads to an increased isolation of the overall household from employment. This is in part due to the sharp disincentives to the partner staying in work, built into the welfare benefits system. Second, while there may be some increase in extra-household sociability with long-term unemployment, this is accompanied by a marked change in the nature of social networks. These become increasingly networks of the unemployed, with little capacity to offer material or psychological support. As a result of these changes both within the household and in external social networks, the long-term unemployed are increasingly locked into their position and cut off from the types of information and assistance that could bring them back into employment. It seems unlikely that national level policies could make much impact on this process of progressive social isolation. Rather it points to the need for a much more widespread development of local community initiatives that could help to integrate the unemployed into local life, construct bridges between the worlds of employment and unemployment, and provide the informational and social resources that are needed if people are to find work.

CHAPTER 7

SOCIAL PROBLEMS AND PERSONAL TROUBLES: UNEMPLOYMENT AND PSYCHOLOGICAL DISTRESS IN IRELAND

Christopher T. Whelan

Introduction

'The primary objective of this Chapter is to turn . . . personal troubles and concerns into social issues . . . and problems open to reason' (Mills, 1959: 86). Our concern with the impact of unemployment on psychological distress is connected to an interest in the more general issue of the mental consequences of acute and chronic stress. The approach adopted reflects the manner in which recent work on the consequences of unemployment has developed closer ties with some of the concerns of psychiatric epidemiology. This broader perspective directs attention to the nature of underlying mechanisms, highlights the impact of broader socioeconomic conditions and facilitates the identification of vulnerable groups. Such concerns are reflected in our desire to connect our analysis of the consequences of unemployment to the wider issue of the impact of poverty.

Employment and unemployment in the Republic of Ireland

Unemployment in Ireland must be viewed in the context of a failure, since the founding of the state, to create jobs on a scale sufficient to cater for its potential growth in employment. Despite this failure Irish unemployment rates for much of the post-independence period were lower than might be expected as a consequence of emigration and the large share of the work force in self-employment. In the period since 1958 the state has sought to create employment growth through industrial policy and the direct creation of public sector employment. Industrial policy concentrated on encouraging investment by export-oriented foreign-owned manufacturing. Although substantial public expenditure was devoted to promoting industrialisation, the strategy was one of indirect job creation with relatively little state control over manufacturing development.

Despite the resources devoted to job creation, unemployment in Ireland has come to be characterised by a high overall rate of unemployment. Currently over one in six workers is unemployed and nearly half of all registered unemployed males have been out of work for more than 2 years. While state policies failed to overcome the obstacles to full employment it did help to reshape the class structure. The rapidity with which the occupational structures changed after 1960 ensured that the decline in opportunities in the traditional sectors was not compensated for by gradual expansion of alternatives. The situation of the unskilled manual group has been exacerbated by the fact that, while the jobs that were lost required less skills and were predominantly located in urban areas, the new jobs required greater levels of skill and were widely dispersed throughout the country. This fact is reflected in the strikingly high rates of unemployment among the non-agricultural unskilled manual working class. Evidence from a representative national sample of over 3000 households showed that close to 60 per cent of men aged between 20 to 64 in the unskilled manual working class were either unemployed or permanently unable to work due to illness or disability. Moreover class origin continued to have an impact even when allowance was made for current class situation. Thus, while one in three of those from non-working-class backgrounds who are currently in the unskilled manual class are out of work, the figure rises to two of three for those from a manual background (Whelan et al., 1992).

Class and poverty

That poverty in economically advanced societies is to be defined in relative terms is now widely accepted. The most commonly used formulation of such a concept in recent years defines poverty as exclusion arising from lack of resources (Townsend, 1979). The approach to measuring poverty we adopt is one which focuses on households that are experiencing both extreme deprivation and are at relatively low income. Income alone is insufficient because it may represent a temporary or atypical situation while life-style indicators are insufficient because we need to establish not only that people live as if they are poor but that they are forced to (Ringen, 1987, 1988). In measuring low income we have chosen a threshold of 70 per cent of average disposable household income adjusted for household size. The life-style element of our poverty measure, which was identified on the basis of theoretical and statistical considerations, we refer to as primary deprivation and comprises items that capture the extent to which people experience deprivations in terms of lack of food, heating, clothing and sufficient money to pay crucial bills (Whelan *et al.*, 1991).

Individuals are defined as poor only if they reside in a household which is experiencing an enforced lack of one or more of the primary life-style items and whose income falls below 70 per cent of average disposable income adjusted for household size (Callan *et al.*, 1993). This measure was developed using data from a specially designed household survey carried out in the Republic of Ireland in 1987. The survey included over 3000 households and almost 7000 individuals. The results of the survey showed that just less than one in five of the Irish adult population were living in households below the poverty line. A strong relationship exists between unemployment and poverty with 44 per cent of the unemployed falling below the poverty threshold in comparison with 16 per cent of the remainder of the sample. The impact of unemployment though varies by class background, with one in ten of those unemployed in the professional and managerial class experiencing poverty compared to close to one in two of those in the manual class. The foregoing evidence suggests that in assessing the impact of unemployment on psychological distress it is necessary to take into account the degree to which the risk of unemployment varies by social class and the extent to which the effects of unemployment are a consequence of its association with poverty.

Unemployment and psychological distress

A variety of studies, cross-sectional macro and longitudinal, converge in establishing the casual impact of unemployment on psychological distress (Warr, 1987; Kessler *et al.*, 1987; Liem, 1987). In cross-sectional comparisons of people who are unemployed with similar people who are in paid work the possibility arises that the differences in levels of psychological distress, which have consistently been observed, may indicate the operation of prior characteristics independent of employment status (Feather and O'Brien, 1986; Vaillant and Vaillant, 1981). The latter interpretation is clearly a great deal more plausible during periods of very low unemployment, when personal characteristics might be thought to impede job-getting. When unemployment rates are high, however, it is more likely that the observed differences arise primarily from the decline in mental health occuring after job loss. (Warr, 1985, 1987). Support for this argument is provided by evidence from a Dutch study (Spruit *et al.*, 1985), which excluded respondents who were identified as having prior health problems that might have led to their unemployment. Despite this control, significant mental health differences were found between the unemployed and a control group of employees. Similarly, there is considerable evidence that unemployed people who regain a job show a rapid and substantial improvement in mental health (Jackson *et al.*, 1983; Payne and Jones, 1987).

Furthermore, a recent study has provided evidence that far from impeding job-seeking efforts, high distress was actually associated with a slightly increased likelihood of finding a new job over the one-year follow-up period (Kessler *et al.*, 1989: 654). Longitudinal studies make particularly clear the causal impact of unemployment and a variety of such studies have now confirmed this effect (Liem, 1987; Warr, 1987).

The data available to us in the Irish case are cross-sectional and we do not wish to deny that there are limitations associated with such data. The information available to us, however, does offer some significant advantages. We are in a position to take into account the effects not only of unemployment but also of social class, income, and lifstyle, and the manner in which personal and social resources mediate between such factors and mental health. This analysis can be conducted not just for the unemployed individuals but also for their family members. This is particularly important in view of the fact that although there is widespread recognition that unemployment brings both economic and psychological problems to the people affected by it, consideration of the relationship between the problems is quite remarkably rare (Kelvin and Jarrett 1985: 18). Such analysis can also make a significant contribution to our ability to choose between competing explanations of the nature of the relationship between unemployment and mental health.

The main measure of psychological distress we employ is the General Health Questionnaire (GHQ) in its twelve-item format. The GHQ was designed by Goldberg (1972) as a screening test for detecting minor psychiatric disorders in the community. If the results of a set of GHQ scores are compared with an independent psychiatric assessment it is possible to state the number of symptoms at which the probability that an individual will be thought to be a psychiatric case exceeds one half. In the case of the twelve-item version the threshold score is two and all respondents scoring above this level will be classified as suffering from psychological distress. Using the GHQ measure we find that just over one in three of the unemployed come above the psychological distress threshold compared to one in fourteen of employees. The differentials between these groups on the individual items are documented in Table 7.1. Almost 36 per cent of unemployed men give a response in the pathological category to the question regarding feeling unhappy and depressed. Over 20 per cent or more in each case indicate that they have felt they couldn't overcome their difficulties; lost much sleep over worry; felt constantly under strain; or had been losing confidence in themselves.

Length of unemployment

The concept of stages of unemployment which emerged in the literature of the 1930s has become a basic concept in accounts of the psychological effects of unemployment. Eisenberg and Lazarfeld, 1938, p. 378) concluded:

We find that all writers who have described the course of unemployment seem to agree on the following points: first there is shock, which is followed by an active hunt for a job, during which the individual is still optimistic and unresigned; he still maintains an unbroken attitude.

Second when all efforts fail, the individual becomes pessimistic, anxious and suffers active distress: this is the most crucial state of all. And third the individual becomes fatalistic and adapts himself to his new state but with a narrower scope. He now has a broken attitude.

Studies relating length of unemployment to mental health have been far from consistent. Our own results show little difference in psychological well-being between those employed for less than a year and those unemployed more than one year. These results are consistent with other findings in the literature. However, this contrast conceals some interesting differences. If those seeking their first job and those on state training schemes are excluded, the data show that levels of mental health decline beyond the second year of unemployment. Severe psychological distress increases from 37 per cent among those unemployed for less than 2 years to 43 per cent among those between 2–3 years and to 54 per cent among those above between 3–4 years. At this point the proportion drops dramatically to 25 per cent for those unemployed more than 4 years. With the exception of this final result, our findings are consistent with the hypothesis of a gradual decline in psychological well-being. See Figure 7.1.

The explanation of this latter finding requires that we turn our attention to the relationship between unemployment and poverty. It is important to keep in mind, as Kelvin and Jarrett (1985:26) stress that 'the

Table 7.1
Indicators of psychological distress among unemployed and
employed

	Unemployed %	Employed %		Unemployed %	Employed %
Been feeling unhappy and depressed	34,2	9,5	Not felt capable of making decisions about things	10,2	2,6
Felt you couldn't overcome your difficulties	22,8	5,7	Not been feeling reasonably happy all things considered	17,9	5,5
Been thinking of yourself as a worthless person	13,8	0,8	Not been able to face up to your problems	13,8	3,6
Lost much sleep over worry	19,5	5,7	Not felt able to enjoy your day to day activities	13,0	2,8
Felt constantly under strain	23,5	11,3	Not felt that you are playing a useful part in things	20,1	2,4
Been losing confidence in yourself	20,0	3,6	Not been able to concentrate on what you are doing	6,0	1,1

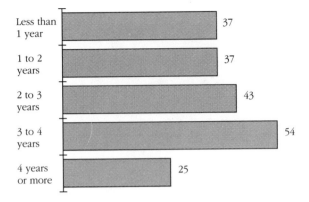

Figure 7.1: Percentage above the psychological distress threshold by
length of unemployment (excluding those looking for their first job
or on state employment/training schemes)

description of stages does not itself provide an explanation of the effects
of unemployment: at most it merely provides the first step towards it,
and that only if the description is sufficiently accurate'. What is necessary, they argue, is to isolate the factors that determine the transition
between stages and developments within them. Despite the attention
devoted to stages, Kelvin and Jarrett (1985: 19–30) note that there have
been very few attempts to trace the interaction of the economic and psychological effects of unemployment and to move beyond description
and examine the systematic relationship between increasing poverty and
changing reactions to unemployment.

Again, if we exclude those seeking their first job and those on state
schemes, we can see from Figure 7.2 that the percentage falling below
our poverty line rises steadily from one in three of those unemployed
less than one year to over half those unemployed for more than three
years. ·This result makes our previous finding regarding the relatively
low levels of distress displayed by those unemployed for more than four
years even more perplexing. At the same time it tends to undermine an
explanation of the deviant result in terms of participation in the black
economy. An alternative explanation could be offered in terms of
coping adjustments. Warr and Jackson (1985: 805) identify two particularly important mechanisms of adaptation to a new role and reduced
commitment to finding a new job. This interpretation takes into account

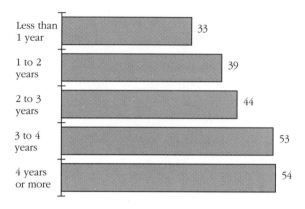

Figure 7.2: Percentage poor by length of unemployment (excluding
those looking for their first job or on state employment/training
schemes)

the fact that the initial period of unemployment may be a particularly
traumatic time, while suggesting that gradual adaptation may take place
in a subsequent phase. A further adjustment arises from the belief that
the probability of obtaining paid work is low; this reduces both employment commitment and job seeking.

Set against such possibilities is the increased probability of poverty
(see Figure 7.2). It seems doubtful to us, in view of the latter, that such
coping strategies could account for the results we have observed. It is
necessary therefore to consider a further possibility raised by Warr and
Jackson (1985: 806) that the type of response alternative employed in
our measure of psychological distress may lead to an underestimation
of levels of distress of those in long-term unemployment. The GHQ may
miss chronic disorders because it asks respondents for an assessment of
symptoms in terms of categories such as 'same as usual'. This seems
to occur less than might be expected on theoretical grounds because
people cling rather stubbornly to the concept of their usual self. It
seems plausible though that those unemployed for more than five years
may have great difficulty in preserving such a concept. It is necessary
to emphasise, however, that, although length of unemployment does
produce some interesting effects, the differences are relatively modest.
Such differences are much less important than the fact of being unemployed (Fryer and Payne, 1986: 253). Similarly, previous unemployment

has a weak effect. Thus a mere 2 per cent more of those at work who had been unemployed in the past 12 months showed severe distress than was the case for those who were at work and had never been unemployed. In relation to the impact of unemployment on physical health, the available evidence suggests that one should avoid an undue emphasis on current spell of unemployment since it diverts attention away from the accumulation of disadvantages over time. With mental health, on the other hand, it does appear that current employment situation is critical. This finding is consistent with the evidence that re-employment leads very rapidly to dramatic improvements in mental health.

Unemployment, poverty and psychological distress

In surveying the current literature on psychological distress a compelling case can be made that its most striking feature is the remarkable lack of emphasis on poverty. A great deal of the literature relating to the impact of unemployment on mental health has operated from a perspective that views levels of distress as influenced by life events with unemployment constituting one such crucial life event. Unemployment is clearly an event which fits readily within the stressful life change approach. The impact on emotional well-being in such cases, arises not from change itself but from change that leads to hardship in basic enduring economic and social circumstances. The most striking example of this process is when unemployment leads to economic hardship and social isolation both for the individual and their family (Pearlin *et al.*, 1981).

When we look at the relationship between poverty and mental health in Irish cases we find that over one in three of the poor come above the psychological distress threshold compared to one in eight of the non-poor. The issue of the relative importance of unemployment and poverty must, to some extent, be an artificial one since unemployment is one of the major causes of poverty. The evidence though is clearly relevant to the issue of the relative significance of manifest and latent functions of employment. Jahoda (1981, 1982) argues that over and above the provision of financial rewards, employment serves a variety of latent functions by embedding the individual in a web of social relations. Our empirical analysis does indeed show that unemployment has a significant effect even among the non-poor, with the unemployed non-poor being five times more likely to come above the threshold of psychological distress than those who are at work or retired. However, our results also clearly

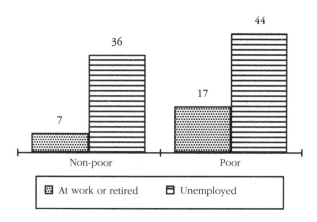

Figure 7.3: The impact of unemployment on the
percentage located above the psychological distress
threshold controlling for poverty

indicate that the impact of unemployment is mediated, to a significant
extent, by exposure to poverty. The cumulative impact of unemployment
and poverty is illustrated by the fact that, while less than one in fourteen
of those at work or of the retired and non-poor exhibited mental health
problems, the figure rose to well over four out of ten for those who
suffer both poverty and unemployment (see Figure 7.3).

Previous work suggests that the impact of unemployment, after controlling for poverty, is likely to be less great among manual workers,
since employment may provide less opportunity for them to relate to
society through their work contributions, to find satisfaction through
achievement or to contribute to some cause. Nevertheless, it may still be
extremely important in terms of enhancement of self esteem, opportunities for sociability, provision of a routine and distraction from personal
problems (Fox, 1976). The importance of such factors is shown by the
fact that, among the manual non-poor only 7 per cent of those at work
or retired were located above the distress threshold, while the figure
rises to 35 per cent of the unemployed. Even if we make allowance
for the fact that we have not controlled for all resource factors, the scale
of the observed difference provides ample support for the rejection of
the view that manual workers are affected entirely by material considerations.

The impact of husband's unemployment on life-style deprivation and poverty

It is clear that while the risk of poverty that is associated with unemployment is one of the important ways in which job loss is translated into psychological distress, a great deal more is involved. Unemployment involves exclusion from a range of experiences and associated psychological benefits, and exposure to the potentially stressful demands of the new role of being unemployed. For the wives of unemployed men the situation is rather different. While their husbands' altered role can clearly have implications for their pattern of activities, any alterations in their own roles are likely to be marginal in comparison with those to which their husbands must accommodate. In view of this we might expect economic factors to loom large. Indeed we do find that husband's unemployment has very little effect when allowance is made for poverty. Where a husband's unemployment does not result in the household being pushed into poverty it does not appear to have any impact on the wife's level of psychological distress. Thus for non-poor households we find that 13 per cent of married women with husbands at work or retired were above the distress threshold, while the comparable figure for those whose husbands were unemployed was 14 per cent. These results do not necessarily imply that a wife's response to her husband's unemployment takes an entirely economic form. However, whatever the emotional aspects of her response are, they do not seem to involve a heightened probability of psychiatric morbidity. Our findings in this regard are consistent with a body of research that has argued that male unemployment may carry a heavy managerial role for wives (Pahl, 1980, 1983).

The buffering effect of social support

It is now generally accepted that the level of distress that people exhibit cannot be adequately predicted from the intensity of the sources of stress, whether the sources be life events or chronic role strains. Instead, people typically confront stress-provoking conditions with a variety of behaviours, perceptions and evaluations that are often capable of mediating the different conditions. Here we are particularly concerned with the role of social support. Our interest is in social support involving flows of affection and emotional concern on the one hand or instrumental and tangible aid on the other.

Our measures of instrumental and emotional support showed that social support of both forms contributes to improved levels of mental health. This issue arises though as to whether support enhances health and well-being irrespective of level of stress or whether its effect operates through buffering the effect of stressful experiences. Our findings provide strong support for the buffering hypothesis. Both support variables have substantial effects but to be understood they must be considered jointly with the role of poverty. Among the non-poor, when we have allowed for the effects of other variables, those lacking social support are more likely to be distressed but the most substantial effects occur for those below the poverty line.

Fatalism and psychological distress

Powerlessness, fatalism, or alternatively mastery has frequently been identified as a vital factor affecting an individual's level of distress. Seeman defined powerlessness as 'the expectancy or probability, held by the individual, that his own behaviour cannot determine the occurrence of the outcomes or reinforcements he seeks' (1959: 784). As Mirowsky and Ross (1986: 26) point out, the importance of powerlessness is recognised in a variety of social and behavioural sciences. Thus, in psychology, the concept of powerlessness appears in a variety of forms, ranging from 'learned helplessness' to 'belief in external control'. The model underlying this approach predicts that, for example, a lower class position will socialise individuals to be more fatalistic in their causal perceptions and that fatalism will increase a person's vulnerability to disorder, primarily because it undermines persistence and effort.

Our measure or fatalism was based on a set of items that have been fairly widely employed (Pearlin *et al.*, 1981):

(i) I can do just about anything I set my mind to.
(ii) I have little control over the things that happen to me.
(iii) What happens in the future depends on me.
(iv) I often feel helpless in dealing with the problems of life.
(v) Sometimes I feel I am being pushed around in life.
(vi) There is a lot I can do to change my life if I want to.
(vii) There is really no way I can solve some of the problems I have.

The evidence shows that a high sense of control among the unemployed is associated with a lower level of psychological distress. This may be explicable by the fact that instrumental coping leads to a search of the environment for potentially distressing conditions, to taking preventive steps, and to accumulating resources or developing skills or habits that will reduce the impact of the unavoidable. In contrast, fatalism leads to ignoring problems until they actually happen (Wheatan, 1983). Lower-class subjects may then carry a triple burden: they are likely to have more problems to deal with: their personal histories are likely to have left them with a deep sense of powerlessness and that sense of powerlessness discourages them from marshalling whatever energy and resources they do have in order to solve their problems. The result for many is a multiplication of despair.

Of course, it is possible to argue that for many deprived respondents, feelings of fatalism are simply an accurate reflection of their environment. They might even be taken as simply reflecting an accurate understanding that their deprivation arises from wider structural factors over which they have no control. Fortunately, a number of items in the Irish survey dealt with perceptions of the causes of poverty. Our analysis shows that there is no significant relationship between fatalism and attribution of poverty to the individual's personal characteristics. This finding suggests that it is possible to facilitate people in developing feelings of personal efficacy without encouraging the tendency to make scapegoats of the deprived.

It has also been suggested that the impact of sense of control on emotional well-being depends on the nature of the preponderant outcomes in one's life. Claiming responsibilities for good outcomes enhances self-esteem while accepting responsibilities for negative outcomes has the opposite effect. Thus for those located at the bottom of the class hierarchy rejecting the role of choice, effort and ability as determinants of life outcomes reduces distress (Hyman, 1986). Despite the intuitive appeal of the theory, as Mirowsky and Ross (1990: 1505) note, the empirical evidence does not support it.

Our own results confirm the findings that increments of control have their most dramatic effect among those with low status and limited resources. Thus not only is the impact of unemployment on psychological distress reduced when we control for fatalism, but it is the unemployed who benefit most from reductions in fatalism. However, it also provides support for the notion of a threshold of dysfunction beyond which point increased feelings of control are actually detrimental to one's well-being. It is necessary to strike a balance between realism and optimism. The optimum level of sense of control is directly related to power and command over resources. The sense of control which is most beneficial to young professional workers who experience little in the way of life-style deprivation would be completely inappropriate for an unemployed manual worker living in a household in which basic items of food, heat and clothing are gone without. Our results, however, confirm the view that most people at all levels of status are likely to benefit from enhanced feelings of control.

Policy implications

The starting point of this chapter was the connection between personal troubles and social problems. The nature of unemployment in Ireland is such that it must be understood in terms of deep-rooted structural problems arising in a peripheral, late industrialising society. As a consequence of such problems and the nature of the policies pursued by the Irish state, unemployment has come to be disproportionately concentrated in particular social classes and most especially among the unskilled working class. Thus problems of unemployment, social exclusion and poverty are ultimately related.

Our study has shown the substantial effect of unemployment and poverty on psychological distress. The extent to which the impact of unemployment is mediated by economic stress and deprivation varies by group. Economic factors are important for all groups, but for married women the unemployment of their spouses has its major effect on their mental health through the grinding consequences of poverty. For others such effects are added to by the damage to their self-esteem brought about by the fact that they are denied the opportunity to undertake roles that are deemed appropriate by society, and are excluded from valued categories of experience, which are associated with employment. The results we have presented clearly demonstrate the role of poverty in mediating the impact of unemployment not only for the individuals affected but for other members of their families. It is important, however, not to replace a one-sided emphasis on the latent functions of employment with claims for the exclusive importance of economic deprivation. Unemployment continues to have a substantial and damaging effect on the psychological health of the unemployed individual even when we control for poverty. Employment does indeed provide more than money. The vast majority of those in employment can enjoy those benefits, while at the same time being fortunate enough to escape the psychological damage associated with exclusion from the customary life style of their society.

Psychological distress arises from the loss of the employment role and/or the experience of a level of deprivation that, by any reasonable standards, must be judged to be extreme. The evidence clearly shows that a great deal of psychological distress could be ameliorated, in principle, by remedial action arising from social policy. Those who experience re-employment or are removed from poverty will regain their mental health. There is a great deal to be said for stressing, as Jahoda (1988: 20–21) does, that what is involved is 'mental health' rather than 'mental illness' in the sense that remedial action must take the form of changing the social circumstances of those affected rather than the provision of individual treatment or therapy.

Increasingly attention is being focused on the need to devise systems of income support that would allow recipients the possibility of perceiving themselves, and being perceived, as making a useful contribution to economic and social life. Recent examples of moves in that direction in Ireland include schemes allowing certain categories of unemployed people to take up a paid part-time job for under 24 hours a weeka and continue to receive an income supplement; pre-retirement allowances for the long-term unemployed aged 60 and over, and a scheme to encourage the unemployed to take an active part in voluntary and community work.

While the role of factors other than poverty and unemployment is clearly secondary, our results do support the view that social support can play an important buffering role. Furthermore, the evidence on the relationship of distress to feelings of fatalism suggests the possibility of intervention, which could ameliorate psychological distress through increasing self-esteem and altering fatalistic attitudes. Our findings also suggest that this could be achieved without the need to impose on the participants an oversimplified view of their situation.

Kane (1987: 405) notes that there has been a reluctance to discuss possible motivational deficits among the poor out of fear of becoming involved in blaming the victim. It is possible, however, to view motivation as the outcome of a complex set of interactions in which restricted opportunity plays a central role. Psychological theory predicts that when faced with uncontrollable circumstances people ultimately respond with learned helplessness. Kane (1987: 416) suggests that there are three such basic messages to be derived from such an analysis. First any motivational deficit observed among the persistent poor should not be thought of as an immutable personal pathology. Second, at the same time, someone who has been conditioned with a lack of control will not necessarily respond immediately to any new opportunities for control. Third, government can play a role, through making real options available in the way of jobs and education – and just as important in making voluntarism salient as an opportunity for control

This analysis is consistent with the view that, while local action cannot in itself solve problems of poverty and disadvantage, it can make a significant contribution to strategies to combat disadvantage (Chanan and Vos, 1990: 31). The difficulties of successful intervention, however, must not be underestimated and can be illustrated by a consideration of the potential role of social support. While our results show that social support can play an important buffering role, even spatial or social concentration of problems do not necessarily encourage collective rather than individual solutions to problems. For many unemployed people, unemployment is perceived as a transitory state and the unemployed may be seen as a reference group in which membership is both unwilling and temporary. The unemployed are defined by what they are not: 'unemployment does not provide the psychological basis for making "The Unemployed" a group with which one identifies, even when the label fits, and when one uses it to describe oneself' (Kelvin and Jarrett, 1985:126). Thus mobilising the unemployed, in a manner which allows them to provide support for each other, is no easy task.

Finally, it must be stressed that many supporting ties depend on adequate funding of basic social and income maintenance programmes (Schilling, 1987: 24). Social networks do not exist in a vacuum, they need resources (Dooley and Catalano, 1985). The balance of research findings suggest that the poor have weaker networks than others. Reciprocity is a central factor in informal networks. When exchange is perceived as being unequal, withdrawal tends to occur (Chanan and Vos, 1990: 39). Many aspects of communal life are linked to workplace characteristics and may exclude the unemployed. Among the unemployed, most mutual aid and support appears to occur between households experiencing unemployment (Morris, 1987).

There would appear to be value in an explicit recognition of this reality, and in encouraging community development responses which recognise the relevance of resource and support issues, and which have the potential to give the unemployed access to categories of experience previously denied to them. But, despite the potential value of local initiatives, it is necessary to stress that the major factors involved in raising levels of psychological distress are the absence of jobs and a minimally acceptable standard of living; the issues involved are clearly national rather than local. The most effective ways to increase self-esteem and feelings of mastery, and to improve mental health are to create jobs and remove people from poverty.

CHAPTER 8

THE FORMATION OF A NEW UNDERCLASS: TRANSITIONS TO AND FROM UNEMPLOYMENT IN THE NETHERLANDS

Paul M. De Graaf and Wout C. Ultee

This chapter examines the thesis that high unemployment during the 1980s made for a new underclass in the Netherlands. We begin by touching on the new underclass as a political issue and a sociological concern in the Netherlands during this period. We then examine the questions addressed in this chapter; in doing so we consider the labour market histories of each partner within a couple between 1980 and 1986. The chapter ends with a discussion of the empirical results obtained.

The underclass as a political issue and a sociological concern

'Dutch society is about to break up.' These words were spoken by Joop Den Uyl in the Dutch parliament in the autumn of 1984. The unemployment rate had climbed to 17 per cent, the highest since the end of World War II. The leader of the Social-Democratic opposition continued: 'Ever deeper cleavages are emerging between those who have a job and those who are excluded from the labour process, between those assured of a higher income and those with a falling standard of living, between those with the chance to take part in new technological and economic developments and those for whom the gate to the future seems closed.' Response from members of the Liberal-Christian coalition came swiftly. The Christian-Democrat De Vries held that so long as people form part of intermediary groups such as the family, the church and voluntary organisations, the consequences of individual unemployment remain limited because these associations contribute to societal stability. The Liberal Zoutendijk maintained that the mobility between unemployment and employment, despite the high overall unemployment rate, remained high.

Sociologists were quick to adduce evidence supporting or refuting these statements by politicians, but when the unemployment rate started falling the social consequences of high unemployment aroused little further interest in parliament. However data now available for the whole of the 1980s seemed to confirm Den Uyl's remarks and the press began using the term underclass.

Of course, when the unemployment rate in the Netherlands fell in the second part of the 1980s, the chances of the unemployed finding a job increased. But to what extent? Official unemployment statistics have shown that the chance of the employed losing their jobs fell even more strongly (Ultee, 1986; Ultee *et al.*, 1992). The two effects taken together mean that the mobility between unemployment and employment decreased. Indeed, mobility in 1989, with a 10 per cent unemployment rate, was decidedly lower than in 1984, when unemployment peaked. A hard core of long-term unemployed had formed.

The first studies of the consequences of unemployment on daily life were cautiously optimistic (Becker *et al.*, 1983; Jol & Van Beek, 1986). In the early 1980s membership of voluntary organisations hardly differed between unemployed and employed, car ownership was only somewhat lower for the unemployed, although their chances of an annual holiday were appreciably lower. By the end of the 1980s the position of the unemployed in all three respects had deteriorated in a relative sense: car ownership for the unemployed fell (remaining the same for the employed), their probability of going on holiday remained the same (increasing for the working population), while membership of voluntary organisations decreased (remaining the same for the employed). Whereas the unemployed at the end of the 1980s were less dissatisfied with the functioning of democracy in the Netherlands than they were in the mid-1980s, the dissatisfaction of the employed had decreased further. In fact, in 1980 the income of an unemployed person was rather more than 60 per cent of that of a person with a job, whereas in 1989 it was well under 50 per cent. In addition, unemployment became more and more concentrated among persons with low school achievement.

Further qualitative research among those unemployed for over two years in areas of high unemployment in some of the larger cities of the Netherlands brought to light the extent to which societal norms were breaking down (Engbersen, 1990). Fewer than half were still actively looking for a job. By way of contrast, more than 10 per cent of those included in surveys did casual jobs while drawing welfare benefit or, by their own admission, played the system in order to obtain higher allowances.

One theme that has remained understudied in sociological research on high unemployment in the Netherlands is its concentration within households. In the next section we examine this phenomenon – as well as that of mobility – and seek to answer questions raised.

The problem addressed

Every month Dutch newspapers publish official figures of unemployed persons. More detailed information is compiled by government agencies with a view to implementing specific policies to combat unemployment. It is common practice in the Netherlands to establish the relation between (un)employment and individual attributes. Such cross-sectional data show that high unemployment during the 1980s particularly affected women, low school achievers, and the youngest and oldest groups in the labour force. While focusing on unemployment in the Netherlands in the 1980s, the questions addressed in this chapter differ in two ways from the usual ones.

First, we do not look at the relative frequency of being unemployed or employed, but at the relative frequency of becoming unemployed after holding a job, and of finding a job after being unemployed. There are two arguments for directing questions at labour market transitions.

To begin with, a high and stable gross unemployment rate can accompany substantial individual mobility between employment and unemployment. If mobility is frequent, no underclass develops. While the relevance of questions as to mobility were recognised early on in discussions about high unemployment and the possible emergence of an underclass, these questions remained understudied. Cross-sectional data cannot settle the question of the extent to which consecutive sets of unemployed persons consist of the same individuals, and longitudinal data were in short supply.

Another argument for directing attention to transitions rather than states is that longitudinal data yield insights which cross-sections cannot provide. The process behind the finding that unemployment is less frequent among men seems obvious: women are more often dismissed, and men have less difficulty in job seeking because employers practise (statistical) discrimination against women. Explaining the positive association between education and unemployment, as found in cross-sectional investigations, appears less easy. It is possible that those with higher educational attainment are as likely to face dismissal as those with lower, but it seems that the chances of finding a job are positively related to education. Certainly this is to be expected when discharge is due to firms and trades going out of business, and when employers prefer highly qualified personnel. But a contrary explanation seems equally plausible. Education may offer a protection against becoming unemployed, yet a higher degree of educational attainmment does not necessarily produce a corresponding vacancy. The cross-sectional relation between age and unemployment can be accounted for in yet another way. Existing regulations about sequence of dismissal tend to protect older employees from unemployment However, given that an older person is unemployed, he or she may have a lower chance of finding another job than someone younger. Such hypotheses about underlying processes, which are relevant to the issue of an emerging underclass, can only be tested by longitudinal research design.

The second way in which our questions diverge from previous ones is that they concern couples, whether partners are married or unmarried, rather than the individual. Mobility is not only a function of age and education but also of a partner's labour market situation. Indeed, the growth of an underclass is inhibited to the extent that an unemployed person's partner is employed. We test hypotheses on partner effect not only to complete earlier explanations of individual transitions, but also to expand on previous research into the question of whether and why unemployment occurs in couples.

Research into couples in the Netherlands has been undertaken using cross-sectional data. The Central Bureau of Statistics (CBS) collects labour force data for households. Analysis of a tabulation crossing the labour market situation of partners from the 1985 CBS Labour Force Survey reveals that a person is more likely to be unemployed when his or her partner is also unemployed (Ultee et al., 1988). This association established, explanations involving matching background characteristics were tested. It is implausible that the decision as to choice of partner is based solely on whether or not one's prospective partner has a job. There is however known to be a strong positive association between the educational attainment of partners in the Netherlands. Since it is also known that education and employment are positively related, an association between the labour market situation of partners is to be expected simply as a by-product of these other relations. Subsequent analysis in fact showed that the actual association between the labour market state of partners is stronger than that predicted with this by-product hypothesis (Ultee et al., 1988). There would seem to be other reasons for unemployment occurring in couples. This issue is pertinent to the larger one of the emergence of an underclass, and it is taken up in this chapter by way of testing for the presence of partner effect. Does the labour market state of the partner influence an individual's labour market mobility? Are the chances of an unemployed female partner finding a job more dependent upon the labour market state of the male partner than if the reverse is the case?

Hypotheses

Six sets of hypotheses explaining a person's labour market mobility in terms of individual attributes, characteristics of partner and contextual properties, will be used to guide our exploration on the formation of a new underclass.

The first set of hypotheses involves the factors that have been found to be important predictors of labour market transitions in cross-sectional research. The most important variables here are respondent's age and education, and the age of respondent's children. To these, we add a variable for the time a person has been in a labour market state. For instance, we want to examine whether it becomes increasingly difficult for a person to get a job the longer they have been unemployed. The stronger this duration effect, the faster the tendency for an underclass to emerge.

A second set of hypotheses brings in partner characteristics. It posits that partners have a common financial goal, and that this leads to compensating activities. When one partner becomes unemployed, total household income decreases, increasing the probability that the other will find a job, if he or she is unemployed, and increasing the likelihood that the other will keep a job, if he or she is employed. If other conditions remain unchanged, this hypothesis follows from the new home situation (Becker, 1981). This type of partner effect is termed substitution effect. To the extent that substitution occurs, it would curb the development of an underclass. Sexton (1988) searched for evidence of substitution but did not find it. Moreover, according to data from the EC Labour Force Sample Survey, the longer a man is unemployed, the lower the probability that his wife will have a job.

A third set of hypotheses assumes that partners have their own goals and that these are independent. But it predicts a positive association between the labour market state of partners, with partners sharing a similar situation of employment or unemployment, as an effect of shared restrictions. An instance of shared restrictions is the tight or slack state of labour markets. An analysis of cross-sectional couples data for the USA included the unemployment rate for the fifty states making up the Union (Ultee *et al.*, 1988). We add regional unemployment rates to our analysis for the Netherlands. Hypotheses about the restrictions partners share run counter to the thesis of an emerging underclass.

A fourth set invokes not shared restrictions but identical resources. It predicts a positive relation between the labour market state of partners as a by-product of individual resources that were matched in the marriage market and the dependence of labour market position on individual resources. Unemployment comes in couples to the extent that partners are similar in educational attainment, with higher levels of education reducing vulnerability to employment. If this by-product explanation holds, high employment does not add to the formation of an underclass.

A fifth set postulates social rather than individual resources, and more precisely, partner effects resulting from the pooling of resources. According to neo-classical economists, eduction primarily represents qualifications affecting productivity in the work setting. The by-product explanation rests on this assumption. In contrast, some sociologists hold that education also represents capacities that can be deployed in other settings. An individual may benefit from a partner who is highly qualified for the labour market, because that partner brings in more information on available jobs, is helpful in writing convincing applications, or gives better advice on how to prevent dismissal. When partners support one another in this way, education is not only human capital (Becker, 1964), but also social capital (Bourdieu et al., 1973). A similar argument leads to the prediction that having a partner in employment is itself a social resource. Just being employed brings with it information not available to others. For brevity's sake we call the positive effect of partner's education on an individual's labour market mobility a *cross effect*; and that of partner's labour market state for an individual's mobility a carry-over effect. Both these partner effects indicate the presence of an underclass.

A sixth set of hypotheses maintains that each partner has her or his own goal, but raises (or lowers) it when the other is (un)successful in the labour market. If preferences depend in this way on the labour market position of a partner, it is predicted that an unemployed female is more likely to find a job when her partner has one, and that a working male is less likely to keep a job when his partner is without one. Interdependence of preferences (Kapteyn, 1985) is difficult to distinguish from carry-over effects. But interdependent preferences foster the emergence of an underclass.

Data

The Dutch data used in this chapter were collected in 1985 and 1986 by the Organisation for Strategic Labour Market Research. Every adult in the households sampled was interviewed unless (s)he was studying, or on military service, or older than sixty. The career of a respondent was mapped starting from January 1980. Individuals were reinterviewed in 1986. To offset panel attrition, new households were added.

We used data on all male/female couples living together, whether officially married or not, so long as the available information satisfied the following conditions:

1. Both partners to be older than 20 and younger than 55. This selection criterion was applied for every month in the period under investigation. It was thus possible that a couple only began to satisfy this condition in course of time, and could also disappear from the sample after a certain period.
2. Information on the education of both partners to be available. This was coded into five categories: the lowest level contains respondents with at most primary education; the second those with certificates in lower vocational or general secondary education; the third category represents those with qualifications in middle vocational or higher secondary education; the fourth stands for persons with higher vocational training; and the fifth for respondents who have completed university courses.
3. To include information about the presence and age of children. The analysis distinguished partners with children up to three years old from among other partners.

These parameters provided 2051 couples. All labour market transitions between January 1980 and January 1986 were mapped for the 4102 individuals involved. Transitions between three states were recorded: employed, unemployed, and not in the labour force (meaning mostly housewife). The exact month was known for each transition.

Techniques of analysis

Our analysis of the determinants of labour market transitions employs event history techniques (Blossfeld et al., 1989). They predict the probability that an event will occur, and estimate effects of predictor variables in regression-like models. The events in our case are mobility from employment to unemployment, from unemployment to employment. Our predictor variables are attributes of the respondents, characteristics of the partner and children, and contextual properties.

Several of our predictor variables are time-dependent covariates: the values for duration, age, age of children, and partner's labour market state can change over time. This dependency is handled by choosing a discrete time model from the 'family' of event history techniques. Blossfeld *et al.* (1989) refer to the basic idea of discrete time models as episode splitting. This procedure divides the total period into each and every possible separate time unit. In our case, we use the month as the minimum time interval, and we computed the exact value of predictor variables for every month. The advantage of episode splitting is that time-dependent covariates can be included; the disadvantage is that the number of cases increases dramatically. Instead of the initial 2051 couples, we now have 120,000 'month couples', after eliminating episodes where information is missing.

Labour market transitions: male partners

The prime question to be tackled in this section is whether the male partner's transitions between employment and unemployment depend on the labour market state of the female partner, and if so, in what way. Other possible transitions, such as those between employment and 'not being in the labour force' are neglected. We did not have enough male partners making this transition in either direction. Apart from the female partner's labour market state, we include the predictor variables mentioned in earlier sections. Since the young and the old may be disadvantaged on the labour market, we include both a linear and a quadratic age effect. Table 8.1 gives resulting models.

We begin with the transition from employment to unemployment. The OSA data set contains 141 such transitions out of a total of 82,800 couple months in which the male partner was employed at the beginning of a month. The first step in the analysis is to include only the female partner's labour market state as a predictor of the probability of her partner becoming unemployed. It is clear that the chances of a man losing his job are indeed higher when his partner is unemployed than when she is employed.

We then introduced the other variables in the analysis, the effect of this being that, even when other factors are controlled for, the chances of becoming unemployed for men whose partners are unemployed remain higher than for men whose partners are employed. This confirms that there are partner effects, but they are effects that lead to increased similarity of labour market position rather than to one partner entering employment to compensate for the fact that the other is out of work. It is clear also that the higher a man's educational attainment, the

Table 8.1

Labour market situations of male
and female partners between 1980 and 1986:
figures obtained monthly (N = 119,835 notings for 2051 couples
in which each partner is between 20 and 55 years old)

		Situation of male-partner		
		Employment	Unempl.ment	Out of employment
Situation of female-partner	Employment	44 982 (40,8 %)	1 887 (38,7 %)	1 528 (31,9 %)
	Unempl. ment	4 162 (3,8 %)	379 (7,8 %)	87 (1,8 %)
	Out of employment	61 029 (55,4 %)	2 605 (53,5 %)	3 176 (66,3 %)
		(100 %)	(100 %)	(100 %)

Source: OSA, 1985–1986

less his likelihood of becoming unemployed, whereas his partner's level of attainment has no bearing on this probability. The age effect is not linear; the likelihood of becoming unemployed increases in the case of younger and older male partners, while those between 35 and 40 are least likely to encounter job loss. And in their case, age of children has no effect at all on this likelihood. When the regional unemployment rate is higher so also is the probability of job loss. This effect is not entirely trivial: the brunt of higher unemployment may be borne by women or by male newcomers to the labour market. Finally, the duration effect is unmistakable. The longer a male partner has been employed, the less his likelihood of becoming unemployed.

Next we examine the effect of different factors on the transitions of male partners from unemployment to employment. There were 111 events out of a total of 3601 couple months where the man was unemployed at the beginning of the month. Again one observes an effect of the woman's labour market state. When she is employed, he has a greater chance of finding work than when she is outside the labour force. But this effect disappears after controls are added for other variables. This indicates that the relationship between one partner's labour market status for this transition is a by-product of the similarity between partners in their individual characteristics; whether the woman is in employment or not makes no direct difference to the man's labour market experience. It should also be noted that there is no hint of a substitution effect, whereby one partner enters employment in order to compensate for the fact that the other does not have a job.

Most of the other variables we examined had little effect on the likelihood of the male partner finding a job when unemployed. But there is a clear duration effect: the longer the man is unemployed, the smaller his chances of finding a job. There is also the anticipated effect of the regional unemployment rate. Remarkably enough, educational attainment does not have a direct impact on the chances of leaving unemployment. It reduces the chances of job loss for male partners, but does not contribute directly to better chances of finding work. Finally, although being middle-aged appears to help a person keep a job, it does not help in finding one.

Labour market transitions: female partners

There are four types of transition between labour market states that occur sufficiently frequently in our data for female partners to permit analysis. First, mobility from employment to unemployment; second, mobility from unemployment to employment; third, transitions from employment to not being in the labour force; and finally, transitions from not being in the labour force to employment.

First we look at the transition from employment to unemployment. The results make it clear at once that a woman's chances of losing her job are also conditioned by her partner's labour market state. The probability that a woman will lose her job is higher when her partner is unemployed. If the data for women are compared with the data for men examined earlier, the effect of a partner's employment status appears to be greater for women than for men. It appears that the presence of young children does not make it more likely that a woman will lose her job. Neither are the chances of job loss affected by higher regional unemployment or by a woman having spent a shorter time in her current job. Nor does a woman's age, her educational attainment and that of her partner produce any effect.

The analysis next turns to the factors that affect a woman's transition from unemployment to employment. The probability of this type of transition depends too on the labour market position of the male partner: she will find a job more readily if he is employed than if he is unemployed. A woman's educational attainment as that of her partner is found to have no effect. In addition, the duration of a current spell of unemployment, the level of regional unemployment and the presence of small children would not appear to affect the chances of getting a job. Age effect, however, is significant and linear: the likelihood that a woman finds employment decreases the older she gets.

As for the two other transitions: to begin with, the male partner's labour market situation does not affect the move from employment to leaving the labour force. There are indeed hardly any significant effects from any of the factors that have been examined. However the positive effect of the duration of a person's experience of employment is noteworthy: the longer the woman has been working, the greater her chances of moving out of the labour force.

Finally, it appears that the transition from a position out of the labour force to employment is not affected by the labour position of the male partner. In contrast, the woman's educational attainment does have a direct effect here: women with a higher level of educational attainment have greater chances of finding a job than do those with a lower. Women who have been out of the labour force for a shorter time also have greater chances of finding employment. The effect of the age of children is as expected: women with young children who are out of the labour force are less likely to become employed than are those in a similar situation without young children. The regional unemployment rate does not affect the likelihood that people will move from being out of the labour market into employment.

Conclusion

Analysis of the labour market histories for both partners, married or unmarried, in the Netherlands from 1980 to 1986 revealed that a person's mobility from one labour market state to another depends on his or her partner's labour market position. There was some indication that the effect of the labour market state of a woman's partner on her transition rate was greater than that of a man's partner on his mobility chances. However, the exact way in which one partner's labour market position might affect the other's labour market transition remained unclear. We adduced social capital explanations: having an employed partner provides access to information about the labour market. On the other hand, a partner's education did not affect labour market mobility.

Did high unemployment in the Netherlands during the 1980s contribute to the emergence of an underclass? Given the results of our event analysis, the answer is a qualified yes. First, the expected duration effects were found in several of the labour market transitions studied. The longer a person has been in a given labour market state, the less the likelihood of his or her leaving it. Second, there appeared to be no tendency for one partner to enter employment in order to compensate for the other being out of work, but several carry-over effects, which showed a tendency for partners' labour market situations to become similar over a period of time. When one partner is unemployed, the likelihood of the other becoming unemployed is greater than if both are in employment. Third, the effects of other predictors on transitions showed a remarkable pattern. Factors such as high educational attainment and middle age make it more likely that employed males will keep their jobs, but they do not directly help them to find a job. One result told strongly against the emergence of an underclass: the educational attainment of a person's partner had no direct influence on that person's mobility chances. This finding was obtained on all transitions studied. Hence any conclusion that there are cultural effects that indicate the emergence of an underclass have to be regarded as very tentative.

CONCLUSION: TOWARDS A NEW UNDERCLASS?

Duncan Gallie

The second part of this book shifts the focus from the causes to the consequences of unemployment. What are the implications of unemployment for the quality of people's material, psychological and social lives? There are three broad interpretations, that are of central interest here. The first, which might be termed the neo-liberal view, conceives of unemployment as to a large extent the outcome of people's choices. In particular, it is argued that people become and remain unemployed because they see little financial advantage in employment, as a result of the high level of welfare benefits that they are entitled to in the welfare state societies that emerged in the aftermath of World War II. The fact that unemployment reflects choice implies that it involves a relatively low level of experienced deprivation. Indeed, a core conclusion of such arguments is that the unemployed do not experience sufficient deprivation. The neo-liberal perspective leads to the advocacy of a reduction of financial support for the unemployed, so that they are subject to increased pressure to find work.

The second perspective views unemployment as involving a major sharpening of class deprivation. It has been seen that vulnerability to unemployment is heavily structured by class, with the unemployed coming predominantly from the manual working class. However class position also can be seen as having major implications for the everyday experience of unemployment. This is most evident with respect to its financial consequences. Where people were previously employed in semi-skilled or unskilled manual work, the low level of their earnings would have made it very difficult for them to have built up any appreciable level of savings. When unemployment strikes, such people have few resources for offsetting the sharp collapse in their income and have to cut back their living standards particularly severely. From the class perspective, income is seen as a fundamental determinant of other aspects of well-being. Poverty, then, leads directly to severe psychological distress, to the breakdown of former patterns of sociability and to social isolation.

Finally, in recent years, there has been a growing tendency to depict the unemployed as coming to constitute an underclass. The popularity of this view may partly reflect the fact that the notion of an underclass can be used in very diverse ways. At a very general level, however, one can detect three common features of most discussions of an underclass. First, it is viewed as a social stratum that suffers from relatively continuous labour market marginality; second, it experiences greater deprivation even than that of the non-skilled manual working class and, third, it possesses its own distinctive sub-culture.

However, at a deeper level, it is clear that different arguments about the underclass reflect quite opposed views about the determinants of membership of the underclass and the cultural characteristics that are associated with such membership. Taking a broad sweep, one can distinguish two fundamentally different conceptions of the underclass. The first, which could be defined as the 'conservative view' attributes unemployment to the personal characteristics and work attitudes of the unemployed themselves. The distinctive characteristic of the unemployed is that they are people who have failed, either because of innate deficiencies or because of a breakdown in the system of primary socialisation, to assimilate the work ethic. They are people who have a degree of behavioural instability that makes it difficult for them to hold any job for long or they are people with a low commitment to employment, the work shy. In placing the responsibility for unemployment primarily on the shoulders of the unemployed themselves, it is a view which shares important common ground with the neo-liberal interpretation. However, the underclass thesis places much less emphasis on immediate financial calculations, and does not suggest that the level of unemployment would be greatly affected by manipulation of the financial support given to the unemployed through the welfare system. Rather, it is accompanied by a somewhat pessimistic view about what can be done for the unemployed. Given that the causes of unemployment are deeply ingrained in long-term, intergenerationally transmitted, subcultural characteristics or inherited personality traits, policy measures are unlikely to be effective in helping people to obtain secure jobs. Further, it differs from the neo-liberal view in placing a much stronger emphasis on the cumulative disadvantage that is associated with unemployment. The deeply set incapacity of members of the underclass to participate in the labour market leads to chronic poverty, which reinforces exclusion both for the current generation and for the children of these families.

CONCLUSION

The alternative or radical conception of the underclass views the unemployed largely as victims of their circumstances. They are victims either of rapid technological development of advanced capitalist societies, with draconian effects on the level skill required of employees, or of the development of employer strategies that increasingly segment the labour market into a core of stable employees that benefit from cumulative advantage and a periphery of highly insecure workers whose jobs are deliberately designed to be discardable in periods of low product demand. The unemployed are essentially people trapped in the secondary labour market, and repeated job loss leads both to deepening poverty and psychological demoralisation.

There is clearly a considerable overlap between the conventional class and the radical underclass views of the consequences of unemployment. In both unemployment is seen as producing sharp deprivation across many aspects of people's lives. The feature that really distinguishes the underclass interpretation is again its emphasis upon the development of a distinctive culture among the unemployed. However, this time, the relevant cultural characteristics are not those of indolence or behavioural instability, they are rather a much sharper level of discontent with the prevailing institutions in society. Locked into a situation of labour market disadvantage, the members of the underclass, it is suggested, become fundamentally disillusioned with the existing political processes, which have failed to ameliorate their situation. Their resentments may be channelled either into political withdrawal, a refusal to participate in conventional politics, or into active support for forms of direct political action. It is a scenario that draws support from accounts of the unemployed in the inter-war period that suggested that they were particularly susceptible to the appeals of extreme left-wing and extreme right-wing political movements.

Unemployment and deprivation

The level of financial deprivation associated with long-term unemployment is likely to be heavily affected by the nature of the welfare regime in the society in question. In practice, there are very wide variations between advanced societies in the type of provision that is available (OECD, 1988).

The countries considered in this volume differ in their unemployment benefit systems in a number of ways. The two principal types of benefit system are insurance based and state assistance schemes. With the exception of Italy, which had no state assistance scheme, all of the countries considered in this volume have a mixture of the two types of system. But these systems differ considerably in terms of the principles upon which payment is made. In particular, they vary in the extent to which they replace income in employment, in the duration of benefits and in their treatment of people's past employment experience as a criterion of eligibility.

For instance, for the initial period of unemployment, France, Spain and the Netherlands offer insurance cover of 70 per cent or more of the income that people were getting when in work. The period that such cover lasts may vary depending upon the length of time that people have been in employment, but, in the most favourable cases, such benefits may last up to 36 months in the Netherlands, 19 months in France, and 12 months in Spain. In Britain, however, even those in their first year of unemployment are paid at a flat rate, with additional allowances confined to the compensation of responsibilities for dependants.

For the long-term unemployed, it is primarily the availability and nature of state assistance that is decisive for the financial deprivation that people are likely to encounter. Thus, for most of the 1980s, there was a sharp division between countries such as the Netherlands, Germany, Britain and Ireland, where the long-term unemployed had the guarantee of a secure if low income for the full duration of time that they were unemployed, and countries such as Spain, Italy (with the exception of workers that benefited from the cassa integrazione) and France, where the very long-term unemployed could be totally deprived of resources.

The argument that the financial deprivations of long-term unemployment is a thing of the past is most likely to be applicable to those countries that have developed a financial safety net for the unemployed that is unlimited in time. Chapters 6 and 7 examine the validity of this view in countries with relatively favourable institutional arrangements for the unemployed, Britain and Ireland. Their conclusions are remarkably similar. The financial costs of unemployment remain very severe in objective terms and this was reflected in people's own accounts of the difficulties they encountered. In Britain, the average disposable income of a person that became unemployed fell to only 59 per cent of their income when in work almost immediately after they had lost their job, and this led to a sharp reduction in people's living standards. They then stayed at this reduced level of expenditure for the remaining duration of their period of unemployment. In Ireland, 40 per cent of the unemployed fell below the poverty threshold as measured by a combination of income and life-style measures. Moreover, there was a steep increase in poverty as the duration of unemployment increased – from a third of those unemployed for less than a year to over half of those unemployed for more than three years. In short, even in those societies with the most favourable type of provision for the long-term unemployed, it is clear that extended unemployment leads to a level of impoverishment that makes any argument about the lack of financial incentives to work seem highly implausible.

For both of these societies, there was also very consistent evidence that unemployment leads to a high level of psychological distress. This was the case both for unemployed men and for unemployed women. It is also a finding that crosses both class and age frontiers. Moreover, both the British and the Irish data show that it is altogether inadequate to restrict consideration of the social consequences of unemployment just to those who are unemployed. For a striking finding is that the distress caused by unemployment spills over to the partners of the unemployed. Indeed, there is some evidence from the British data that the female partners of unemployed men may suffer even more than the men themselves. Further, there is clear evidence that unemployment increases the level of tension in family relations and, indeed, increases the probability that people's marriages will break up.

There has been a considerable debate about which aspects of the experience of unemployment are most important in accounting for the anxiety and depression that people experience. Some have argued that the critical factor is the financial difficulty that accompanies unemployment, whereas others have put the emphasis on non-financial factors, such as the loss of a clear time-structuring to the day or of any sense of involvement in a wider collective purpose. Whelan demonstrates from the Irish data that poverty is a major factor increasing the level of psychological distress among the unemployed, although the fact that unemployment has some psychological effect even among the non-poor suggests that non-financial factors may have a significant secondary role. However, financial deprivation would appear to be the decisive factor explaining financial distress among the partners of the unemployed.

Overall, then, the research reported in this volume confirms those arguments that stress the sharp deprivations that unemployment generates. These affect not only people's living standards, but also their psychological well-being. These effects are not confined to the unemployed themselves, but have major spill-over effects for the partners of unemployed people. It is notable that the evidence for such deprivation has been largely collected in societies with relatively generous financial provisions for the long-term unemployed. It seems probable that the distress that accompanies long-term unemployment will be even greater in those societies when unemployment benefit systems provide a safety net of limited duration.

A sub-culture of the unemployed?

The view that unemployment leads to cumulative disadvantages in people's lives is common to both class and underclass interpretations of unemployment. The major point of divergence between these perspectives lies over the issue of whether the unemployed, and particularly the long-term unemployed, participate in a sub-culture that is markedly different from that of employees. From the perspective of underclass theory, the unemployed display a marked cultural distinctiveness even in comparison to people from the same general occupational background. With respect to the conservative underclass thesis such cultural characteristics should relate primarily to the development of attitudes that reduce people's employability, whereas for the radical underclass thesis they should be reflected in political attitudes that involve the rejection of conventional parliamentary politics.

To take first the conservative thesis, there are a number of different ways in which such cultural distinctiveness might be manifest. It has been noted above that unemployment is associated with much higher levels of psychological distress. The conservative underclass thesis might suggest that this reflects a lower psychological stability of unemployed people that might be a cause rather than a consequence of unemployment. However, a more detailed examination of the research results suggests that this is not a tenable argument. British longitudinal studies have shown that there is a very clear sequence in the relationship between job loss and psychological distress: distress increases sharply after people have lost their jobs and people's psychological well-being improves again once they return to work. There is no evidence that the unemployed are people who suffer from higher levels of psychological instability that makes them difficult to employ.

A second sign of the emergence of an underclass might lie in the tendency of the unemployed to develop self-sufficient social networks, in which the unemployed form a community which provides its members with a positive sense of identity and a degree of social support that permits a viable alternative life-style to that of the employed. The British data certainly show that there is a very marked segregation of the friendship networks of the employed and the unemployed. The longer that a person is unemployed the greater the extent to which their friendship network is dominated by other unemployed people. But do such networks provide the basis for a viable, or even attractive, alternative life style? The evidence suggests clearly that they do not. For the people that are involved in networks of other unemployed people at the same time report exceptionally low levels of social support. They are more likely to feel that they have nobody to assist them if they are feeling depressed and they are less likely to feel that they can rely on anybody else for material assistance. This suggests that the social segregation of the unemployed reflects primarily the way in which redundancies can hit whole local communities and exclusion through stigma or lack of resources for reciprocity, rather than preference for an alternative life style. Social segregation is best perceived as another of the cumulative disadvantages that results from unemployment.

Third, in Chapter 8 on the Netherlands, De Graaf and Ultee suggest that there may be some evidence of the growth of an underclass in cases where both partners in a household are unemployed. While such cases represent a relatively small proportion of the unemployed as a whole, it is notable that, across a wide range of different societies, there is a tendency for unemployment to come in households. The important point about this is that it may be indicative of a process of social closure. Where both partners are out of employment, there is a rupture in the flow of communication between the household and the world of employment. It becomes very much more likely that people will become irretrievably locked into their situation of unemployment. This in turn is likely to provide the context for the development of a culture of unemployment that involves different identities and different attitudes to work and society than those that prevail among the employed.

As De Graaf and Ultee point out the fact that partners are both unemployed may reflect a variety of factors and not all of these can be seen as reflecting tendencies for the emergence of an underclass. For instance, both partners may be out of work because they live in an area of particularly high unemployment and are victims of a high rate of redundancy in local industry. Alternatively, both may have low levels of education and their exclusion from employment may simply result from the mismatch between their individual qualifications and the requirements of the new types of jobs that are becoming available. Neither of these explanations imply that the unemployed are becoming part of a separate subculture. De Graaf and Ultee argue that it is only if there is a link between the employment status of both partners after such factors have been allowed for that one can point to evidence of an underclass. It would indicate a household cultural effect, characterised in particular by isolation from the normal information flows about employment opportunities and effective methods of job search. After a careful analysis of the data, they conclude that there is some evidence of such cultural factors at wotk for this particular sub-group of the unemployed.

Finally, turning from the conservative to the radical version of the underclass thesis, what evidence is there that the experience of unemployment leads to the development of distinctive political attitudes? The main source of evidence linking unemployment to political attitudes derives from the inter-war period. It was the research into the impact of unemployment in the Austrian community of Marienthal that provided the striking picture of the descent into complete political apathy of the long-term unemployed. But other analyses linked unemployment to support for extremist political movements of both the right and the left. The most influential elaboration of this view was probably that of Kornhauser. In his theory of mass society he argued that any process that leads to widespread social atomisation, in the sense of dissolving the intermediary groups of society, heightens vulnerability to the appeal of extremist movements of an authoritarian type. Such movements provide a sense of social membership and purpose that is no longer achievable through everyday participation in the society. Unemployment is one of the major sources of social atomisation, undercutting multiple social ties. As he puts it: 'extreme mass movements appeal to the unemployed on psychological as well as economic grounds, as ways of overcoming feelings of anxiety and futility, and of finding new solidarity and forms of activity' (Kornhauser, 1960: 167).

There has been considerable debate about the precise links between unemployment and extremist politics in the inter-war period. It seems unlikely that the type of evidence that would be needed to reach firm conclusions for that period will ever be available. However, in the present period, suitable individual level data can be collected, although the amount of research is in practice still rather slight. In this volume, some relevant research findings are presented for Britain. These conflict sharply with the argument that the unemployed come to reject democratic processes in favour either of political withdrawal or of direct action politics. Once background factors have been controlled for, there is no evidence of greater political apathy among the unemployed. Similarly, it seems clear that unemployment does not generate radical political ideologies that seek major upheavals in the institutional system. Rather what emerges from the evidence is a consistent picture whereby the experience of unemployment strengthens people's attachment to collectivist welfare values and consolidates support for the traditional party of the left. Unemployment then increases aspirations for social reform, but it is for reform within a democratic framework.

In short, the chapters in this book demonstrate that unemployment sharply heightens deprivations both of a material and psychological type. There is no support for the view that, with the rise of the welfare state, the unemployed can maintain a standard of living that is likely to discourage them from seeking employment. Even in welfare systems that provide relatively favourable provision for long-term unemployment, people experience a very sharp reduction in their income and living standards.

Yet, while exposed to severe multiple deprivation, the evidence would not suggest that, in general, the unemployed become a culturally distinct group in the way suggested by the different versions of underclass theory. It is only the minority of the unemployed that are in households where both partners are unemployed that show signs of becoming a quite distinct social stratum. For the majority, unemployment involves a sharp aggravation of class disadvantage and it is responded to by a heightening of people's attachment to collectivist values.

SELECT BIBLIOGRAPHY

Accornero A., 1987 'La novità è l'incoccupazione di massa', *Rivista trimestrale*, 1–2.

Accornero A. and Carmignani F., 1986, *I paradossi della discopuzione*, Bologna, Il Mulino.

Agnès M., Coppieters C., Foudi R., Stankiewicz F. and Vanecloo N., 1985, 'Les chômeurs de longue durée: disparités des revenus et distance à l'emploi', *Travail et Emploi*, 26: 23–33.

Bakke E. W., 1933, *The unemployed man*, London, Nisbet.

Barnett C., 1986, *The audit of war: the illusion and reality of Britain as a great nation*, London, Macmillan.

Barrère-Maurisson M. A. and Merle V., 1982, 'Marché du travail, chômage et répartition des travailleurs (l'exemple des travailleur depuis longtemps au chômage)', *Economie et Société*, **16**, 10: 1041–1088.

Becker, G., 1964, *Human Capital*, New York, Columbia University Press.

Becker J. W., Vink R. & Wiebrens C., 1983, *Opvattingen van werklozen 1974–1982*, Rijswijk, Sociaal en Cultureel Planbureau.

Benoît-Guilbot O., 1985, 'Acteurs sociaux, politiques de l'emploi et structures du chômage: le jeu du mistigri', *Futuribles*, 84–85: 15–42.

Benoît-Guilbot O., 1987, 'Les structures sociales du chômage en France et en Grande-Bretagne, influences sociétales', *Sociologie du travail*, 2: 219–236.

Benoît-Guilbot O., 1990, 'La recherche d'emploi: stratégies, qualification scolaire ou professionnelle et "qualification sociale"', *Sociologie du travail*, **32**, 4: 491–506.

Bentolila S. and Blanchard O., 1990, 'Spanish unemployment', *Economic Policy*, 10: 233–281.

Bettio F. and Villa P., 1989, 'Non wage work and disguised wage employment in Italy', *Economia e Banca-Annali scientifici*, 21.

Blanchflower D. G., Millward N. and Oswald A. J., 1991, 'Unionism and employment behaviour', *The Economic Journal*, **101**, 407: 815–834.

Bloch F., Buisson M. and Mermet J. C., 1991, 'L'activité féminine: une affaire de familles', *Sociologie du travail*, **33**, 2: 255–275.

Blossfeld H. P., Hamerle A. and Mayer K. U., 1989, *Event history analysis;*

statistical theory and application in the social sciences, Hillsdale N. J., Lawrence Erlbaum Associate.

BMA, 1990, Bundesminister für Arbeit und Sozialordnung (eds), *Arbeitsvermittlung zwischen Arbeitslosigkeit und Fachkräftemangel*, Abschlußbericht zum Forschungsprojekt: Arbeitsuche, berufliche Mobilität und soziale Lage Arbeitsloser, Forschungsbericht nr 197, Bonn.

Bonss W. and Heinze R. G. (eds), 1984, *Arbeitslosigkeit in der Arbeitsgesellschaft*, Frankfurt, Suhrkamp.

Bourdet Y. and Persson I., 1991, 'Politique de l'emploi et durée du chômage: une comparaison franco-suédoise', *Observations et diagnostics économiques*, 38: 65–93.

Bourdieu P., Boltanski L. and Saint-Martin M. de, 1973, 'Les stratégies de reconversion', *Social Science Information*, 12: 61–113.

Breen R., Hannan D. F., Rottman D. and Whelan C. T., 1990, *Understanding contemporary Ireland*, London, Macmillan.

Brenner M. H., 1973, *Mental illness and the economy*, Cambridge Mass., Harvard University Press.

Brinkmann C., 1984, 'Die individuellen Folgen langfristiger Arbeitslosigkeit. Ergebnisse einer repräsentativen Längsschnittuntersuchung', *Mitteilungen aus der Arbeitsmarkt- und Berufsforschung*, 4: 454–473.

Brinkmann C., Friedrich D., Fuchs L. and Lindlahr K. O., 1991, 'Arbeitslosigkeit und Sozialhilfebezug. Sonderuntersuchung der kommunalen Spitzenverbände in Zusammenarbeit mit der Bundesanstalt für Arbeit im September 1989', *Mitteilungen aus der Arbeitsmarkt- und Berufsforschung*, 1: 157–177.

Brinkmann C. and Potthoff P., 1983, 'Gesundheitlicher Probleme in der Eingangsphase der Arbeitslosigkeit', *Mitteilungen aus der Arbeitsmarkt- und Berufsforschung*, 4: 378–394.

Brittan S., 1975, 'Second thoughts on full employment policy', London, Centre for Policy Studies.

Büchtemann C., 1984, 'Der Arbeitslosigkeitsprozeß. Theorie und Empirie strukturierter Arbeitslosigkeit in der Bundesrepublik Deutschland', in: Bonss. and Heinze R. G. (eds), *Arbeitslosigkeit in der Arbeitsgesellschaft*, Frankfurt, Suhrkamp.

Buttler F. and Cramer U., 1991, 'Umfang und Ursachen von mis-match-Arbeitslosigkeit in Westdeutschland', *Mitteilungen aus der Arbeitsmarkt- und BerufsforschungMittAB*, 3.

Callan T., Hannan D., Nolan B., Whelan C. T. and Creighton S., 1989, *Poverty and the social welfare system in Ireland*, Dublin, Economic and Social Research Institute, Paper n° 146.

Callan T., Nolan B. and Whelan C. T., 1993, *Resources, deprivation and the measurement of poverty*, Oxford, Oxford University Press.

Catalano R. A. and Dooley C. D., 1983, 'Health effects of economic instability: a test of economic stress hypothesis', *Journal of Health and Social Behavior*, 24: 46–60.

Cebrian I., Garrido L. and Toharia L., 1991, 'Los parados de larga duración y la protección social', in: Pérez Yruela M. and Moreno L. (eds), *Política social y Estado del bienestar*, Madrid, Ministerio de Asuntos Sociales, Colección Estudios.

Cebrian I., Garrido L. and Toharia L., 1992, 'El paro de larga duración en España', in: Inem, *El problema del paro de larga duración*, Madrid, Inem.

Cezard M., 1986, 'Famille, milieu social et risque de chômage', *Economie et Statistique*, 193–194: 91–96.

Chanan G. and Vos K., 1990, *Social change and local action: coping with disadvantage in urban areas*, Dublin, European Foundation for the Improvement of living and working Conditions.

Coeffic N., 1984, 'Chômage et famille', *Données sociales*: 81–84.

Cohen S. and Leonard Symes S., 'Issues in the study and application of social support', in: Cohen S. and Leonard Syme S. (eds), *Social support and health*, London, Academic Press.

Conseil Économique et social, 1991, 'Le chômage de longue durée', rapport présenté par R. Leray, *Journal officiel de la République française*.

Cornilleau G., Marioni P. and Roguet B., 1990, 'Quinze ans de politique de l'emploi', *Observations et diagnostics économiques*, 31: 91–120.

Corpeleyn A., 1975, 'Arbeidskrachtentelling 1975, enige gegevens over de arbeidsmobiliteit', *Sociale Maandstratistiek*, 25: 886–896.

Cramer U., Karr W. and Rudolph H., 1986, 'Über den richtigen Umgang mit der Arbeitslosen-Statistik', *Mitteilungen aus der Arbeitsmarkt- und Berufsforschung*, 3: 409–421.

Dahrendorf R., 1988, *The modern social conflict*, London, Weidenfeld and Nicolson.

Daniel W. W., 1990, *The unemployed flow*, London, Policy Studies Institute.

Déchaux J. H., 1990, 'Pauvretés ancienne et nouvelle en France', *Observations et diagnostics économiques*, 30: 7–33.

Denny K. and Nickell S., 1991, 'Unions and investment in British manufacturing industry', *British Journal of Industrial Relations*, 29.

Dietz F., 1988, 'Strukturwandel auf dem Arbeitsmarkt. Entwicklung bei den sozialversicherungspflichtig beschäftigten Arbeitnehmern nach Wirtschaftszweigen, Berufen und Qualifikationen zwischen 1974 und 1986', *Mitteilungen aus der Arbeitsmarkt- und Berufsforschung*, 1: 115–152.

Dirven H. J., Lammers J. and Ultee W. C., 1990, 'Werkend en toch economisch afhankelijk? Net uurloon van werkende gehuwde vrouwen en dat van hun werkende echtgenoot in Australie, Canada, Hongarije, Nederland, Tsiechoslowakije, de Verenigde Staten en West-Duitsland rond 1980', *Sociale Wetenschappen*, 32: 61–93.

Dooley D. and Catalano R., 1985, 'Why the economy predicts help-seeking: a test of competing explanations', in: Wescott G. Svensson P. G. and Zollner H. F. K. (eds), *Health policy implications of unemployment*, Copenhagen, WHO.

Ehrens B. and Hedges B., 1990, *Survey of incomes in and out of work*, London, Social and Community Planning Research.

Eisenberg P. and Lazarsfeld, P. F., 1938, 'The psychological effects on unemployment', *Psychological Bulletin*, 35: 358–390.

Engbersen G., 1990, *Publieke bijstandsgeheimen, het ontstaan van een onderklasse in Nederland*, Leiden, Stenfert Kroese.

Fagin L. & Little M., 1984, *The forsaken families: the effects of unemployment on family life*, Harmondsworth, Penguin Books Ltd.

Feather and O'Brien G. E., 1986, 'A longitudinal study of the effects of employment and unemployment on school leavers', *Journal of Occupational Psychology*, 59: 121–144.

Fernandez F., Garrido L. and Toharia L. 1991, 'Empleo y paro en España, 1976–1990', in: Miguélez F. and Prieto C. (eds), *Las relaciones laborales en Espana*, Madrid, Siglo XXI.

Field F., 1989, *Losing out, the emergence of Britain's underclass*, Oxford, Basil Blackwell.

Flap H. D. and De Graaf P., 1986, 'Social capital and attained occupational status', *The Netherlands Journal of Sociology*, 22: 145–161.

Flinn C. and Hechman J., 1983, 'Are unemployment and out of the labor force behaviorally distinct labor force states?' *Journal of Labor Economics*, 1: 28–42.

Florens J.P., Fougère D. and Werquin P., 1990, 'Durées de chômage et transitions sur le marché du travail', *Sociologie du travail*, 32, 114, 439-468.

Fox A., 1976, 'The meaning of work', Occupational categories and cultures I, *People and work*, Milton Keynes, Open University.

Freyer D., 1986, 'Employment deprivation and personal agency during unemployment', *Social Behaviour*, 1: 3-23

Gallie D., 1988, *Employment in Britain*, Oxford, Blackwell.

Gallie D. and Vogler C., 1990, 'Labour market deprivation and collectivism', *European Journal of Sociology*, 31, 1.

Gallino L., 1985, *Il lavoro e il suo doppio*, Bologna, Il Mulino.

Gelot D., 1989, 'Le chômage de longue durée en évolution', *Grand angle sur l'emploi*, 4: 5-17.

Gérard-Varet L.A., Joutard X., Teyssier G. and Werquin P., 1990, 'Durée du chômage et trajectoires individuelles vis-à-vis des marchés du travail. Deux études sur données micro-économiques', Greque, Rapport PIRTTEM-CNRS.

Goldberg D.P., 1972, The detection of psychiatric illness by questionnaire, Oxford, Oxford University Press.

Goldthorpe J.H., 1980, *Social mobility and class structure*, Oxford, Clarendon Press.

Goldthorpe J.H., Lockwood D., Bechhofer F. and Platt J., 1968, *The affluent worker*, Cambridge, Cambridge University Press.

Groupe International De Politique économique De L'ofce (Atkinson A. B., Blanchard O.J., Fitoussi J. P., Flemming J.S., Malinvaud E., Phelps E.S., Solow R. M.), 1992, *La Désinflation compétitive, le mark et les politiques budgétaires en Europe*, Paris, Seuil.

Granovetter M., 1974, *Getting a job*, Cambridge Mass., Harvard University Press.

Harris J., 1972, *Unemployment and politics: a study in English social policy 1886-1914*, Oxford, Clarendon Press.

Heady P. and Smyth M., 1989, *Living standards during unemployment*, vol. 1, London, HMSO.

Heath A., 1981, *Social mobility*, London, Fontana Press.

Heath A., *et al.*, 1991, *Understanding political change. The British voter 1964-1987*, Oxford, Pergamon Press.

Herpin N., 1990a, 'L'insertion professionnelle, le chômeur et ses deux familles', *Données sociales*: 76–79.

Herpin, N. 1990b, 'La famille à l'épreuve du chômage', *Economie et Statistique*, 235: 31–41.

Herpin N., 1992, *Les conséquences du chômage sur la consommation*, forthcoming.

Heseler H., 1990, 'Stabile und instabile Erwerbsverläufe bei Betriebsstillegungen', in: Dressel W. u. a., *Lebenslauf, Arbeitsmarket and Sozialpolitik*, BeitrAB 133, Nürnberg.

Hess D., Hartenstein W. and Smid M. 1991, 'Auswirkungen der Arbeitslosigkeit auf die Familie', *Mitteilungen aus der Arbeitsmarkt- und Berufsforschung*, 1:178–192.

Huyghes-Despontes H., 1990, 'A partir du chômage, quels itinéraires pour quels chômeurs?', *Sociologie du travail*, 32, 4, 411–438.

Infratest, 1989, *Arbeitssuche, berufliche Mobilität und soziale Lage Arbeitsloser*, München, Infratest.

Ingram P.N., 1991, 'Changes in working practices in British manufacturing industry in the 1980s; a study of employee concessions made during wage negotiations', *British Journal of Industrial Relations*, 29, 1:1–13.

Iribarne (d') P., 1990a, *Le Chômage paradoxal*, Paris, PUF.

Iribarne (d') P., 1990b, 'Formes nationales de vie en société et chômage des années quatre-vingt', *Sociologie du travail*, 32, 4: 561–574.

Jackman R., Layard R. and Savouri S., 1990, 'Labour market mismatch: a framework for thought', Centre for Economic Performance, London, London School of Economics, Discussion Paper, no. 1.

Jackson P. R., Stafford E. M., Banks M. H. and Warr P. B., 1983, 'Unemployment and psychological distress in young people: the moderating role of employment commitment', *Journal of Applied Psychology*, 68: 525–535.

Jacobi O. and Müller-Jentsch W., 1990, 'West Germany: Continuity and structural change', in: Baglioni G. and Crouch C. (eds), *European industrial relations, the challenge of flexibility*, London, Sage Publications.

Jahoda M., 1981, 'Work, employment and unemployment: values, theories and approaches in social research', *American Psychologist*, 36: 184–191.

Jahoda M., 1982, *Employment and unemployment: a social-psychological analysis*, Cambridge, Cambridge University Press.

Jahoda M., 1988, 'Economic recession and mental health: some conceptual issues', *Journal of Social Issues*, 44, 4: 13–24.

Jahoda M., Lazarsfeld P. F. and Zeiss H., 1971 (1933), *Marienthal: the sociology of an unemployed community*, New York, Aldine Atherton.

Jimeno J. F. and Toharia L., 1992, *Unemployment and labour market flexibility: Spain*, Genève, BIT.

Jol C. and Van Beek P., 1986, 'De nieuwe tweedeling – ook op sociaal en politek terrein?' *Economisb-Statistische*, 71: 14–17.

Joutard X. and Werquin P., 1990, 'Un traitement paramétrique de l'assurance-chômage sur données longitudinales UNEDIC', Document de travail Greque.

Kane T. J., 1987, 'Giving back control: long term poverty and motivation', *Social Service Review*, 61, 3: 405–419.

Kapteyn A., 1985, 'Utility and economics', *De Economist*, 133: 1–20.

Karr W. and John K., 1989, 'Mehrfacharbeitslosigkeit und kumulierte Arbeitslosigkeit', *Mitteilungen aus der Arbeitsmarkt- und Berufsforschung*, 1: 1–16.

Kasl S. and Cobb S., 1979, 'Some mental health consequences of plant closings and job loss', in: Ferman W. A. and Gordus J.P. (eds), *Mental health and the economy*, Kalamazoo ML, The Upjohn Institute.

Kelvin P. and Jarrett J. E., 1985, *Unemployment: its social psychological effects*, Cambridge, Cambridge University Press.

Kessler R., Blake Turner J. and House J. S., 1989, 'Unemployment, reemployment and emotional functioning in a community sample', *American Sociological Review*, 54: 648–657.

Kessler R., House J. S. and Blake Turner J., 1987, Unemployment and health in a community sample', *Journal of Health and Social Behaviour*, 28: 51–59.

Keynes J. M., 1964 (1936), *The general theory of employment, interest and money*, London, Macmillan.

Klauder W., 1990, 'Auswirkungen der politischen und wirtschaftlichen Entwicklung seit 1989 auf die Arbeitsmarktperspektiven', *Mitteilungen aus der Arbeitsmarkt- und Berufsforschung*, 1: 22–33.

Kornhauser W., 1960, *The politics of mass society*, London, Routledge and Kegan Paul.

Korpi W., 1991, 'Political and economic explanations for unemployment a cross-national and long-term analysis', *British Journal of Political Science*, 21: 315–348.

Lampard R., 1990, 'An examination of the relationship between marital dissolution and unemployment', Social Change and Economic Life Initiative, Working paper n° 17.

Layard R., Nickell S. and Jackman R., 1991, *Unemployment, macroeconomic performance and the labour market*, Oxford, Oxford University Press.

Liem R., 1987, 'The psychological consequences of unemployment: a comparison of findings and definitions', *Social Research*, 54: 321–353.

Lindbeck A. and Snower D., 1985, 'Explanations of unemployment', *Oxford Review of Economic Policy*, 1.

McKee L. and Bell C., 1985, 'Marital and family relations in times and male unemployment', in: Roberts B., Finnegan R. & Gallie D. (eds), *New approaches to economic life*, Manchester, Manchester University Press.

McKee L. & Bell C., 1986, 'His unemployment, her problem: the domestic and marital consequences of male unemployment', in: Allen S. *et al.* (eds), *The experience of unemployment*, London, Macmillan.

Marshall G., Rose D., Newby H. and Vogler C., 1988, 'Political quiescence among the unemployed in modern Britain', in Rose D. (ed), *Social stratification and economic change*, London, Hutchinson.

Marshall J. R. and Funch D. P., 1979, 'Mental illness and the economy: a critique and partial replication', *Journal of Health and Social Behavior*, 20: 282–289.

Maruani M., Reynaud E. and Romani C., 1989, *La Flexibilité en Italie: débats sur l'emploi*, Paris, Syros Alternatives.

Maurice M., Sellier F. and Sylvestre J. J., 1979, 'La production de la hiérarchie dans l'entreprise: recherche d'un effet sociétal. Comparaison France-Allemagne', *Revue française de sociologie*, **21**, 2: 175–191.

Mayer H. L., 1990, 'Entwicklung und Struktur der Erwerbslosigkeit Ergebnisse des Mikrozensus und der EG-Arbeits-kräftestichprobe', *Wirtschaft und Statistik*, 1: 16–30.

Miles I., 1983, *Adaptation to unemployment?*, Occasional paper n°. 20, Falmer, Sussex, Social Science Policy Research Unit, Sussex, University Press.

Mirowsky J. and Ross C., 1986, 'Social patterns of distress', in: Turner R. & Short J. J. Jnr (eds), *Annual Review of Sociology*, vol. 12.

Mirowsky J. and Ross C., 1990, 'The consolation prize theory of alienation', *American Journal of Sociology*, **95**, 6, 1505–1535.

Morris L. D., 1987, 'Local social polarisation: a case study of Hartlepool', *International Journal of Urban and Regional Research*, **11**, 5, 331–350.

Moylan S., Miller J. and Davies R., 1984, *For richer for poorer? DHSS cohort study of unemployed men*, London, HMSO.

OECD, 1987, *Employment Outlook*, Paris, OECD

OECD, 1988, *Employment Outlook*, Paris, OECD

OECD, 1989, *Economies in Transition, structural adjustment in the OECD countries*, Paris, OECD.

OECD, 1990, *Employment Outlook*, Paris, OECD.

OECD, 1991, *Employment Outlook*, Paris, OECD.

Pahl J., 1980, 'Patterns of money management within marriage', *Journal of Social Policy*, 9: 313–335.

Pahl J., 1983, 'The allocation of money and the structuring of inequality within marriage', *Sociological Review*, 31: 235–262.

Payne J., 1987, 'Does unemployment run in families? Some findings from the General House Survey', *Sociology*, **21**, 2: 199–214.

Payne R. and Jones J. G., 1987, 'Social class and re-employment: changes in health and perceived financial circumstances', *Journal of Occupational Behavior*, 8: 175–184.

Payne R. L., Warr P. B. and Hartley J., 1984, 'Social class and psychological ill-health during unemployment', *Sociology of Health and Illness*, 6: 153–175.

Pearlin L., Menaghan E., Lieberman M. and Mullan J. T., 1981 'The stress process', *Journal of Health and Social Behavior*, 22: 337–351.

Pilgrim Trust, 1938, *Men without work*, Cambridge, Cambridge University Press.

Reyneri E., 1989a, 'Mercato e politiche del lavoro', in: Cella G. P. & Treu T., *Relazioni industriali*, Bologna, Il Mulino (traduction espagnole, 1991, Madrid, Ministerio de trabajo y seguridad social).

Reyneri E., 1989b, 'The Italian labor market: between state control and social regulation', in: Lange P. and Regini M. (eds), *State, market and social regulation*, Cambridge, Cambridge University Press.

Reyneri E., 1992, *La disoccupazione di lungo periodo in Emilia-Romagna tra marginalità sociale e lavoro precario*, Quaderni dell'Osservatorio sul mercato del lavoro della Regione Emilia-Romagna.

Ringen S., 1987, *The possibility of politics*, Oxford, Clarendon Press.

Ringen S., 1988, 'Direct and indirect measures of poverty', *Journal of Social Policy*, **17**, 93: 351–366.

Ronayne T., Cullen K., Wynne L., Ryan G. and Cullen J., 1986, *Locally based responses to long-term unemployment*, Dublin, European Foundation for the Improvement of Living and Working Conditions.

Rosenbladt B. von, 1991, 'Arbeitslose in einer prosperierenden Wirtschaft', *Mitteilungen aus der Arbeitsmarkt-und Berufsforschung*, 1: 146–156.

Salais R., 1980, 'Le chômage, un phénomène de file d'attente', *Economie et Statistique*, 123: 67–78.

Schilling R. F., 1987, 'Limitations of social support', *Social Service Review*. 19–31.

Schmidt M. G., 1983, 'The Welfare State and the economy in periods of economic crisis: a comparative analysis of twenty-three OECD nations', *European Journal of Political Research*, 11.

Schnapper D., 1981, *L'Epreuve du chômage*, Paris, Gallimard.

Schnapper D., 1989, 'Rapport à l'emploi, protection sociale et statuts sociaux', *Revue française de sociologie*, **40**, 1, 3–29.

Seeman M., 1959, 'On the meaning of alienation', *American Sociological Review*, 24: 783–791.

Ses, 1990, 'Le passage par le 13e mois de chômage', ministère du Travail et de l'Emploi, *Premières informations*, 204.

Sexton J. J., 1988, *Long-term unemployment, its wider labor market effects in countries of the European Community*, Luxembourg, Office for Official Publications of the European Community.

Sibille H. (ed.), 1989, *Les Politiques d'emploi à l'épreuve du chômage de longue durée*, Paris, Syros Alternatives.

Sixma H. and Ultee W. C., 1984, 'Marriage patterns and the openness of society; educational heterogamy in the Netherlands in 1959, 1971 et 1977' in: Bakker B., Dronkers J. and Ganzeboom H. B. G. (eds), *Social stratification and mobility in the Netherlands*, Amsterdam, Siswo.

Solow R., 1991, 'Les Européens ont sacrifié l'emploi à leur compétitivité', débat au colloque 'Agir contre le chômage de longue durée', MIRE, ministère du Travail, *Partenaires*, 21.

Spruit I. P., Bastiannen J., Verkley H., Van Niewenhuijzen M. G. and Stolk J., 1985, *Experiencing unemployment, financial constraints and health*, Leiden, Institute of Social Medicine.

Theeuwes J., Kerkhofs M. and Lindeboom M., 1988, *Toestanden, Overgangen en Duren op de Nederlandse Arbeidsmarkt 1980-1985*, Den Haag, Organisatie voor Strategisch Arbeidsmarktonderzoek.

Thelot C., 1988, 'La sortie du chômage', in: *Mélanges économiques, Essais en l'honneur de E. Malinvaud*, Paris, Economica, éditions Ehess: 862–993.

Thoits P., 1982, 'Conceptual methodological and theoretical problems on studying social support as a buffer against life stress', *Journal of Health and Social Behavior*, 23: 145–159.

Thoits P., 1984, 'Explaining distributions of psychological vulnerability: lack of social support in the face of life-stress', *Social Forces*, 63: 452–481.

Thoits P., 1985, 'Social support and psychological well-being: theoretical possibilities', in: Sarason I. G. and Sarason B. R. (eds), *Social support, theory, research and application*, Lancaster, Martinus Nijhoff.

Toharia I., 1988, 'Los parados en España: cómo los medimos, cuántos hay y cuántos habrá', *Débats*, 25.

Toharia L., 1991a, 'Le marché du travail en Espagne', in: Guitton C., Maruani M. and Reynaud E. (eds), *L'Emploi en Espagne*, Paris, Syros Alternatives.

Toharia, 1991b, 'El paro femenino en España: algunos elementos para el análisis', *Revista de Economía y Sociología del Trabajo*, 13.

Toharia, L. and Fernandez F., 1988, 'Actividad, empleo y paro en España: 1970–1987', *Situación*.

Townsend P., 1979, *Poverty in the United Kingdom*, Harmondsworth, Penguin Books.

Tresmontant R., 1991, 'Chômage: les chances d'en sortir' *Economie et Statistique*, 241: 41–51.

Trew K. and Kilpatrick R., 1983, 'The daily life of unemployed. Social and psychological dimensions', Unpublished final report to the SSRC.

Ultee W., 1988, 'High unemployment and social differenciation', in: Social and Cultural Planning Office, *Social and cultural report 1986*, Rijswijk, Social and Cultural Planning Office.

Ultee W., Arts W. and Flap H., 1992, *Sociologie: vragen, theorieën, bevindingen*, Groningen, Wolters Noordhoff.

Ultee W. C., Dessens J. and Jansen W., 1988, 'Why does unemployment come in couples? An analysis of (non) employment homogamy tables for Canada, the Netherlands and the United States in the 1980s,' *European Sociological Review*, 4: 111–222.

Ultee W. C., Dessens J. and Jansen W., 1990, *Stratificering 1974–1988*, Den Haag, Organisatie voor Strategisch Arbeidsmarktonderzoek.

Vaillant G. and Vaillant C., 1981, 'Natural history of male psychological health X: work as a predictor of positive mental health', *American Journal of Psychiatry*, 136: 1433–1440.

Van der Wee H., 1986, *Prosperity and upheaval: the world economy 1945–80*, London, Viking.

Voisin M. J., 1990, 'Retrouver un emploi après le chômage', *Données sociales*: 72–75.

Warr P. B., 1985, 'Twelve questions about unemployment and health', in: Roberts B., Finnegan R. and Gallie D. (eds), *New approaches to economic life*, Manchester, Manchester University Press.

Warr P. B., 1987, *Work, unemployment and mental health*, Oxford, Clarendon Press.

Warr P. B and Jackson P. R., 1984, 'Men without jobs: some correlates of age and length of unemployment', *Journal of Occupational Psychology*, 52: 129–188.

Warr P. B. and Jackson P. R., 1985, 'Factors influencing the psychological impact of prolonged unemployment and re-employment', *Psychological Medicine*, 15: 795–807.

Warr P. B and Payne R. L., 1983, 'Social class and reported changes in behaviour after job loss', *Journal of Applied Psychology*, 13: 206–222.

Weber M., 1921, *Wirtschaft und Gesellschaft*, Tübingen, Mohr.

Whelan C. T., Breen R. and Whelan B. J., 1992, 'Industrialization, class formation and social mobility in Ireland' in: Goldthorpe J. H And Whelan C. T. (eds), *The development of industrial society in Ireland*, Oxford, Oxford University Press.

Whelan C. T., Hannan D. F & Creighton S., 1991, *Unemployment, poverty and psychological distress*, Dublin, Economic and Social Research Institute, General Research Series, 150.

White M., 1983, *Long-term unemployment and labour markets*, London, Policy Studies Institute.

White M., 1991, *Against unemployment*, London, Policy Studies Institute.

White M. and McRae S., 1989, *Young adults in long-term unemployment*, London, Policy Studies Institute.